The Procrastination Playbook
for Adults with ADHD

from the same author

The Ultimate Time Management Toolkit
25 Productivity Tools for Adults with ADHD and Chronically Busy People
Risa Williams
ISBN 978 1 83997 1 785
eISBN 978 1 83997 1 792

The Ultimate Anxiety Toolkit
25 Tools to Worry Less, Relax More, and Boost Your Self-Esteem
Risa Williams
Illustrated by Jennifer Whitney and Amanda Way
ISBN 978 1 78775 770 7
eISBN 978 1 78775 771 4

The Ultimate Self-Esteem Toolkit
25 Tools to Boost Confidence, Achieve Goals, and Find Happiness
Risa Williams
ISBN 978 1 83997 474 8
eISBN 978 1 83997 475 5

of related interest

ADHD an A-Z
Figuring it Out Step by Step
Leanne Maskell
ISBN 978 1 83997 385 7
eISBN 978 1 83997 386 4

The Procrastination Playbook for Adults with ADHD

How to Catch Sneaky Forms of
Procrastination Before They Catch You

Risa Williams, LMFT

Jessica Kingsley Publishers
London and Philadelphia

First published in Great Britain in 2025 by Jessica Kingsley Publishers
An imprint of John Murray Press

1

Copyright © Risa Williams 2025

The right of Risa Williams to be identified as the Author of the Work has been asserted
by her in accordance with the Copyright, Designs and Patents Act 1988.

A CIP catalogue record for this title is available from the British Library and the Library of Congress

ISBN 978 1 80501 229 0
eISBN 978 1 80501 230 6

Printed and bound in the United States by Integrated Books International

Jessica Kingsley Publishers' policy is to use papers that are natural, renewable and recyclable
products and made from wood grown in sustainable forests. The logging and manufacturing
processes are expected to conform to the environmental regulations of the country of origin.

Jessica Kingsley Publishers
Carmelite House
50 Victoria Embankment
London EC4Y 0DZ

www.jkp.com

John Murray Press
Part of Hodder & Stoughton Ltd
An Hachette Company

Contents

Acknowledgments 9

Part 1: Understanding Procrastination

1. How We Get Ourselves Stuck 13
   When we go blind to time   16
   The procrastination fog   18

2. Three Factors That Affect Motivation 21
   The stress factor   22
   The self-talk factor   27
   The support factor   32

3. Types of Procrastination 35
   Micro- and macro-procrastinations   35
   Helpful and unhelpful procrastinations   37

4. The Procrastination Clouds 43
   Visible forms of procrastination   44
   Subtle forms of procrastination   48
   Reading the signs   57

5. Getting Started 61
   Why do we procrastinate?   61
   The first tiny shift   62
   How to use the worksheets in this book   63

Part 2: Begin Your Journey

The Starting Line 67

Worksheet Checklist 71
What Kind of Procrastination Is It?   73
Time Management Procrastination   78
Time Frames for Goals   82
Task Prioritization   84
Time Mapping   85
First Steps: Goals and Projects   88
Working on Habits   91
First Steps: Micro-Procrastinations   93
Activation Energy   96
Planning Rewards   102
Setting Intentions   105
Avoiding the Task   107
Organizing the Steps   110
Making Decisions   113
Extreme Thinking Glasses   116
The Avoidance Onion   122
Roots of Procrastination   125
What I Can Tell Myself   127
Motivating Self-Talk   130
Different Rules   132
Roots of Perfectionism   137
Facts vs. Feelings   139
The Encouragement List   144
The Finish Line Picture   146
Future-You Letter   148
Half-Way Drift   150
Getting Distracted   153
Where Does Time Go?   154
Time Blocking   156
Time Tracking   161

The Procrastination Signs   171
The Stress Signs   173
Self-Talk Review   175
Accountability Review   177
The Procrastination Round-Up   179

The Finish Line 182

About the Author 185

Mental Health Resources 187

References 189

Acknowledgments

I am so truly grateful for all the support and encouragement provided from these wonderful people as I wrote this book: Zach Smith, Leo and Max Williams, my editor Sean Townsend, Laura Savage and all the amazing folks at Jessica Kingsley Publishers who published my last three books (*The Ultimate Toolkit Book Series*), Holly Daniels and Cassandra Lane for publishing my magazine articles, Eden Byrne, Michael Ian Scott, Sepideh Saremi, Leo Williams, Erica Curtis, Stevon Lewis, and Ezra Werb for reading and testing out the book ahead of time, Dulcie Yamanaka, Jennifer Whitney, and Amanda Way for their beautiful artwork on my other books and planners, Maggie Lynch, Mike Sonksen, Romy, Anton and Veronica Yanagisawa, Kathryn Singer and Tony Smith, Trevor Stockwell, Miguel Lee, Joel Levin, Camille Brown, Dr. Tamara Soles, Dr. Scott Waltman, Dr. Catherine Smith, Dr. Mike Feldmeir, Andrew Lawston, Mollie Volinsky, Hilary Kern, and a really huge thank you to all my wonderful clients and students who have tested out the tools in this book over the years. Thank you to the authors who have inspired me while writing this: David Burns, Dr. Ned Hallowell, Esther Hicks, Brené Brown, Elizabeth Gilbert, Wayne Dyer, Eckhart Tolle, Pema Chödrön, and Thich Nhat Hanh.

And thank you to the thousands of listeners around the globe who have tuned into my podcast, *The Motivation Mindset,* over the last year. Thank you to all the amazing guests and co-hosts I've had on the show. It's been so much fun making episodes with you, knowing that we are reaching people in so many countries who are looking for new strategies and practical tools.

Finally, I am truly grateful to everyone who read my last books, *The Ultimate Time Management Toolkit*, *The Ultimate Self-Esteem Toolkit*, *The Ultimate Anxiety Toolkit*, and *The Motivation Mindset Journal*. Thanks to all the readers who have reached out to me to say how my books have helped you in some way. Your words often gave me the encouragement I needed to keep on writing that next page—thank you so much.

I hope you know how inspiring it is for writers to hear from their readers and to see people leaving reviews. It is often that little boost of motivation we need to write the next chapter ahead.

Never underestimate the power of encouragement. It is one of the most powerful things out there in this world.

I hope this book gives back a little encouragement to someone out there reading it, too. And I hope this book helps you find your way out of procrastination and on your way to everything you really want to do with your time.

To learn more about Risa's books, articles, podcast, and workshops, please visit risawilliams.com and follow her at @risawilliamstherapy.

PART 1

UNDERSTANDING PROCRASTINATION

1

How We Get Ourselves Stuck

Do you often get stuck procrastinating your projects, tasks, and goals? Do you drift off at the mid-point of things and then struggle to get back on track again? Do you feel so overwhelmed by the task in front of you that you don't even know where to begin? Or do you get almost to the end of a goal and then watch as your motivation engine stalls out a few feet away from the finish line?

I can relate to all of these things! I understand what you're going through right now, and I understand the uncomfortable emotions that tend to accompany procrastination, such as guilt, shame, and anxiety, too.

This practical guidebook is here to help you find your way back on track so you can start doing the things you want to do in an easier, calmer, and (hopefully) more enjoyable way.

In this book, you will learn:

* the **three main factors** that can help you manage your procrastination more effectively
* the **different types of procrastination** people tend to get stuck in
* how to read the **internal warning signs of procrastination** so that you can catch them as they're happening to you
* how to **navigate your way out of procrastination** by following the "Choose Your Own Adventure" worksheet journey that I've provided here, so that you can get un-stuck and moving forward again.

I'm the author of *The Ultimate Time Management Toolkit, The Ultimate Self-Esteem Toolkit*, and *The Ultimate Anxiety Toolkit*. I'm also a psychotherapist, a professor, and a time management consultant, who has helped hundreds of people overcome procrastination and achieve their goals. I specialize in ADHD management, burnout reduction, time management tools, and goal-setting strategies, and I'm the host of *The Motivation Mindset*, a podcast about getting stuff done.

All this is to say that I spend a lot of my time talking to people about... *time*.

When you talk to people about time, it leads you to so many other fascinating subjects. What do they want to be doing more of? What do they want to be doing less of? And what do they want to be doing with their time that's meaningful to them in some way?

In other words, we only have so much time on this planet. How do we want to be spending it?

This particular question must be important to you, too; otherwise, you wouldn't have picked up this book. And it's a really good question to ask yourself right now, one that can lead you to insight, inspiration, and *action*.

Over the last decade, I've helped a wide range of people from various backgrounds, occupations, and situations get themselves un-stuck from the grips of procrastination so that they could go on to accomplish truly amazing things. And it's my intention to help you to do the same thing here with this book.

Believe me, I am no stranger to procrastination in my own life. Many years ago, before I developed these tools and started implementing them, I procrastinated writing a book for *five years in a row*.

Yes, you read that correctly. Five years in a row! Don't worry, it wasn't this book that you're reading now (although that would be quite funny). It was one of my very first books, so there were many obstacles that I hadn't learned to navigate yet. The first obstacle was that I had no idea what my own **internal procrastination cues** looked like. As a result, I didn't always fully realize that I was procrastinating *when* I was procrastinating.

Maybe this is true of you as well?

There are times when procrastination is completely obvious to you and everyone else around you. In these cases, it can be easy to admit that you're doing it *when* you're doing it. Sometimes, you might even loudly announce it to people: "Yep, I'm procrastinating! I really don't want to do this thing. So, that's what I'm doing right now. I am definitely procrastinating!"

And then there are other times, when procrastination sneaks up on you slowly, like a thick dark fog that catches you completely off-guard. In these cases, you probably won't openly admit that you're doing it, because you won't even realize that you are!

And that's exactly what happened to me. For five years, I kept telling myself I was making progress on the book because I kept thinking about it, constantly, while I was working, teaching, raising two kids, and doing a lot of other things. In my mind, I figured I'd get around to sitting down and putting it all on paper when I had the "time." But this "time" thing was vague and abstract; it kept stretching on into the future, because there just wasn't a stretch of "time" that presented itself easily in this way.

The truth is, most of us are very busy these days, and most of us have an ongoing list of things we need to do each week that never seems to end. However, it's *also* true that we do have little chunks of time here and there, and if we really want to do something, we make a point to move ourselves forward, even if it's in the tiniest amounts, one small step at a time.

And although I did really want to write the book, I also hadn't even taken the tiniest step forward with it. This became very apparent when I ran into an old friend I hadn't seen for a few years, who casually inquired if I had finished the book. As I listened to myself explain how I hadn't even started writing it yet, I was suddenly struck by the starkness of my own procrastination, staring right back at me, straight in the eyes.

During this moment of intense clarity, I asked myself, "How long has it really been since I first said I was going to write this book?" And I added up the years, to my own shock and amazement. It was then that I realized:

Time really flies when you're avoiding things.

It was as though I had gone into some procrastination time-warp where I had been telling myself I would start writing "tomorrow," and somehow that "tomorrow" had turned into five years of "tomorrows." But it honestly didn't feel as though that much time had passed on the inside of it.

It became altogether too clear that I had stalled out at the starting line, but I wasn't really sure how or why.

When procrastination sets in, that's where the self-investigation can begin.

Instead of beating myself up about it (which would only make the problem worse) or falling back on excuses that there wasn't any "time" (which would only make me avoid it longer), I decided to get really curious. The therapist-me wanted to investigate the situation a little more. What was holding me back? How did this procrastination thing actually work and what was the easiest way out of it?

When we go blind to time

Procrastination tends to make us lose touch with our internal "ticking clock" of time. In this way, we have a feeling of **time blindness,** where we can't correctly gauge how much time has passed.

If you have ADHD, time blindness may be something that happens to you frequently. A 2021 study done by Charles University and Teaching Hospital in the Czech Republic found "evidence that suggests that differences in time perception are a central symptom in adults with ADHD" (Weissenberger *et al.* 2021).

Sometimes, it's possible that on some deeper subconscious level, we procrastinate in order to pause our feeling of passing time. When we're mentally "paused" with a project we're doing, we may also think time is "paused" too, but it really isn't. It's an illusion. Time is *moving*. It's *going*. Whether or not we happen to be in sync with it, it's marching right on down the line.

With or without your awareness of it,
time is always going forward.

So, let's take a deep breath and notice where time actually is right now. Is there something you've also put off "until tomorrow" for too many "tomorrows"?

QUICK JOURNALING EXERCISE

What are some projects or goals that you may have become "time blind" to?

Make a quick list of projects or tasks that you've been putting off for a while. How long have you been procrastinating these things?

1. . . . .

2. . . . .

3. . . . .

4. . . . .

5. . . . .

After realizing I had become lost in some kind of time blindness, I admitted to myself that I wasn't going to write a book if I kept going about it in this way (which was clearly not writing a book). And I became determined to figure my way out of it. However:

We can't solve problems from the same thinking that created the problems to begin with.

That's why the first step to addressing procrastination is to admit to yourself that you are procrastinating.

Say to yourself: "I fully accept that I am procrastinating right now."

Good job! Now you've admitted it to yourself, you can begin to deal with it.

The procrastination fog

Procrastination comes in many shapes and forms throughout our everyday lives. It often sneaks up on us like a gray fog engulfing the ship we are sailing towards our goals, tasks, or projects.

This is why when a **"procrastination fog"** appears, people will often say things like "I have no idea how I got here" or "I don't know how to get moving again" or "I don't know how I got lost here for so long!"

Because once you sail into a low-hanging **procrastination fog**, it can feel very difficult to navigate your way out of it. You can't see forwards and you can't see left or right. You get a little lost for a while, just wandering around your own fog. Which is why I'm here to help with this practical guidebook and map.

Using this book, you will now be able to effectively spot the **"procrastination** clouds" looming over your ship, so you can effectively navigate yourself out of them and toward your intended destination.

THIS GUIDEBOOK CAN HELP YOU:

- **CALL IT OUT** (Notice the warning signs of procrastination clouds and call them out)

- **PLAN IT OUT** (Label the specific type of procrastination and pick a strategy forward)

- **TAKE ACTION** (Make a clear decision to act and take the first step out of there)

Around the time I was working on "naming" my own types of procrastination, I was working with many clients who were also stuck in various **procrastination fogs** themselves. As a result, I discovered that there were only so many types of procrastinations that people tend to get stuck in. And I began to learn, through working with lots of people, which tools worked best for which types of procrastination.

As a result of using these tools, over the last five years I've been able to write *five books in a row*. That's one book per year. Compare this to my previous track record of *zero* books across five years, and you can begin to see how using these tools consistently can really change things for you.

What have I been doing differently? Through practicing the tools in this book and teaching them to others, I have become very sensitive to any signs of procrastination on the horizon.

I am a **pro-active procrastination catcher** now. I catch my own procrastination as it is forming, as much as possible. I never let myself go too deep into procrastination for too long.

I know too much now, and I don't want to get lost in a procrastination fog for another five years.

2

Three Factors That Affect Motivation

So, how can you become a pro-active procrastination catcher? Let's start with the basics.

Before we start breaking down and naming all the **different types of procrastination,** let's look at **three factors** we must address first. These factors tend to affect our general motivation levels, as well as our ability to organize, initiate, and follow through with tasks and goals.

* **The stress factor**
  How we manage our daily stress which can impact our ability to focus on tasks.
* **The self-talk factor**
  How we talk to ourselves about tasks we need to do and our ability to do them.
* **The support factor**
  How we find support and accountability to stay on track with tasks.

By addressing these three factors, you will be setting yourself up to successfully overcome procrastination. As you work your way through this book, you'll gain a solid basis of tools to build upon and use in conjunction with other strategies provided in the worksheets ahead.

The stress factor

Procrastination is **the act of intentionally delaying or postponing something we need or want to do.** It's estimated that 25% of adults are **chronic procrastinators** (Low 2023), and I personally believe that this percentage is only increasing each year. In fact, it's one of the main things I work on with people these days.

Why might procrastination be happening to so many people right now?

In 2019, one-third of people around the world were reporting feeling high levels of stress (a statistic that has been increasing every year since the pandemic) (Gallup 2019), and the United States recently made the list of "most stressed-out countries" with 55% of Americans reporting feeling high levels of stress on a regular basis, according to the American Institute of Stress (2022).

Think of **stress as a magnifier:** if you're already feeling intensely about something, stress will magnify that feeling to a way higher level of intensity. If you're already struggling with **executive functioning skills,** such as task prioritization, organization, or making decisions, stress tends to make those things feel even more challenging for your brain to do.

A study done at Waseda University in Japan found that "evidence also indicates that people with more serious ADHD symptoms experience more procrastination as well as internalizing symptoms" (Oguchi, *et al.* 2021). Additionally, in a study at the University of Göttingen in Germany, researchers gave two participants groups (ADHD and non-ADHD) a stress test and discovered that "consistent with our assumptions in regard to the psychological stress response, the ADHD group experienced significantly greater subjective stress" (Lackschewitz, Hüther, and Kröner-Herwig 2008).

So, if you have ADHD, you may be more prone to procrastination, and you may *also* be more prone to feeling the effects of stress, too.

Research over the last decade has connected chronic procrastination to high levels of stress. According to Professor Fuschia Sirois of Durham University:

Theory and evidence also suggest stress may be a precursor, and not just a consequence, of procrastination. A temporal mood regulation perspective posits that people procrastinate tasks which elicit negative emotional states as a means of regulating their immediate mood through task avoidance. (Sirois 2023)

This "immediate mood regulation," according to Dr. Timothy Pychyl, becomes "a battle between your limbic system and your pre-frontal cortex." Your limbic system tries to give you "immediate mood repair" by taking control of things from the pre-frontal cortex, which handles our executive functioning, such as task prioritization and task initiation (quoted in Jaffe 2013).

In other words, procrastination may manifest as a quick way we are trying to regulate our stress in the moment, only, in reality, we're often just creating more stress for ourselves to experience in the future.

You can think of this **stress/procrastination loop** like this:

STRESS LEADS US TO PROCRASTINATE →
WHICH LEADS US TO FEEL STRESSED →
WHICH LEADS US TO PROCRASTINATE MORE →
AND SO ON...

This is exactly what I'm seeing these days as a therapist. People are experiencing high levels of everyday stress, and, as a result, people are procrastinating more frequently. Which, unfortunately, just tends to stress them out even more, because now they're beating themselves up about procrastinating, and this is how the cycle continues.

Taking this "stress factor" into consideration, prioritizing **regulating our daily stress levels** is essential, because it's going to affect so many other areas of our lives, including our ability to start and finish things we want to do.

Think about how high your stress level tends to get day to day, week to week. At this moment, where would you rate it? Is your stress at a low, middle, or high level right now?

Our stress levels go up and down each day; we aren't always at "high," and we aren't always at "low." It depends on what we're doing and how we're feeling about what we're doing, as well as other internal and external circumstances in that particular moment. It can change day to day, hour to hour, task to task. Because our stress levels are constantly changing, it can be helpful to learn to read our own **"stress signs"** so that we can catch our stress before it starts to get too high.

Internal stress signs are how stress *feels* inside your body and brain, and **external stress signs** are how it *looks* on the outside when you're at a high level of stress. Here are some examples from clients when they start to feel a high level of stress:

INTERNAL SIGNS	EXTERNAL SIGNS
I get headaches.	I start snapping at people and acting grumpy.
I can't stop worrying.	I forget to take a lunch break.
I have a lot of trouble focusing.	I lose my keys and phone a lot; I can't find things.
I grind my teeth.	I keep doing more tasks instead of taking breaks.

Now, when you start to grind your teeth or notice that you've skipped lunch again, you can pause and do a quick check-in with yourself. Ask yourself,

"How high is my stress right now?" Take time to really hear the answer that you receive from your body and brain. And then take a small step to lower your stress in that moment.

Over the last decade, many neuroscience studies[1] have shown that these types of activities tend to help many people regulate their daily stress:

* meditating
* walking
* exercising
* practicing mindfulness
* breathing techniques such as "box breathing" (breathe in for four seconds, hold for four seconds, breathe out for four seconds, hold for four seconds)
* yoga stretches and yogic breathing techniques
* vagal nerve relaxation techniques (stretches, vocalization, humming, chanting)
* being around "green spaces" (such as nature, trees, plants)
* looking at "blue spaces" (oceans, lakes, marinas)
* listening to calming and soothing music
* watching funny shows or movies that make you laugh
* finding relaxing activities that engage your focus (e.g., drawing, journaling, reading, or coloring).

Since everyone finds different things relaxing to do, it can be beneficial to take some time to figure out what works best for your particular brain.

At a deeper level, we may want to deny that the general state of our bodies is affecting our brains and our ability to focus on things. We may have an unstated belief that our brains are functioning completely independently—as though they are drifting far away, lost in thoughts—from what our bodies are doing down below.

The opposite is true; the two are entirely interconnected, and when one

---

1 Akimbekov and Razzaque 2021; Balban *et al.* 2023; Can *et al.* 2020; Kok *et al.* 2013; University of the West of England 2018; White *et al.* 2021.

is feeling exhausted or stressed out, the other is as well. Healthy sleep, exercise, resting, and eating habits all contribute to how much energy we have, physically, mentally, and emotionally. If we spend more time each week intentionally taking care of our bodies, this will *also* benefit our brains, and can often give us that much-needed boost of neural energy to follow through with our tasks and goals.

QUICK JOURNALING EXERCISE

Write out a bullet point list of things you can do to bring your stress down in small notches. Give yourself three to five options you can try when you start feeling stressed out. What things tend to reset your brain? What things tend to reset your body? List them all out!

1. . . . .

2. . . . .

3. . . . .

4. . . . .

5. . . . .

Regulating our stress is essential to managing procrastination. If we want our brains to be able to focus and move forward with things, we need to prioritize bringing our stress down first.

When we intentionally bring down our stress, we are making space and room for our clarity and focus to kick in. We're clearing the path in front of us so that we can see where to go next.

The self-talk factor

As we've just learned, the first factor in managing procrastination is learning ways to regulate our daily stress levels. The second factor is learning how to regulate our daily self-talk, which is how we are talking to ourselves about ourselves, and also about tasks we have to do.

Where does our internal self-talk come from? If you grew up feeling like your brain functioned a little differently from everyone else's (a common feeling for those with ADHD and/or other executive functioning issues), it's also possible you were criticized more than other kids around you. Dr. Michael Jellineck estimates that "a child with ADHD could receive 20,000 corrective or negative comments by the time he or she is age 10" (Jellineck 2010).

Perhaps your parents, guardians, teachers, or other adults around you were delivering these types of messages to you quite frequently when you were younger. Perhaps you often felt more criticized than praised, and it taught you to internalize this pattern with yourself. As self-talk can stem from a variety of interactions and experiences over time, it can be helpful to explore the roots of your own self-talk with a therapist or psychologist in sessions together.

Sometimes, hearing a lot of criticism growing up can lead people to form a harsh **inner critic**, who then repeats these types of internal criticisms long into adulthood as a pattern of thought. Our harsh internal critic may tell us things like "You're not doing it right," "You're so bad at this," "You're an idiot!" or "You're not good enough to do it!" and other mean and unhelpful things, thousands of times per day.

If it's true that we think approximately 6000 thoughts per day (Tseng and Poppenk 2020), and if a big percentage of these thoughts are self-critical ones, it's bound have an impact on our motivation to do things.

Imagine if another person was standing there, watching you do a task, criticizing the way you were doing it the whole time. How would this make you feel? Would you want to continue to do the task? Or would you think, "What's the point of doing this anyway?!"

Now, imagine this person is you!

When it comes to procrastination, our **daily self-talk** can impact these two areas:

* our confidence in ourselves to do the task
* our motivation to complete the task.

As you read the examples below, start to imagine how saying these things internally might impact your **confidence and motivation** to finish a particular task.

Task: **Building a new bookshelf.** Self-talk that will affect **confidence** to do the task:

* "I'm the worst at following instructions and I will never make any sense of these!"
* "I always screw these things up and have to redo them!"
* "The last thing I built is still wobbly and I know I am going to mess this up, too."
* "I'm terrible at tasks that everyone else seems to be able to do."
* "I'm such an idiot!"

Outcome of self-talk: "I don't want to build the bookshelf because I'm going to screw it up."

Self-talk that will affect **motivation** to complete the task:

* "This is taking so long and it isn't fun and I wish I never bought this stupid thing."
* "This bookshelf is a nightmare to build."
* "These are the worst instructions I have ever read—there's no way anyone can follow them!"
* "This is going to take forever and I hate doing this."

Outcome of self-talk: "There is no reward for completing this hard and frustrating task."

Just from reading these few examples, you can start to see how **self-talk** can affect our ability to start a task and our ability to complete it. You can remember it like this:

We can talk ourselves out of doing things easily, by the way that we're talking to ourselves.

To begin to change our **self-talk patterns,** we can work on mixing in a few new soothing, positive, and encouraging phrases to tell ourselves throughout the day. We can start small and build over time. Types of positive and encouraging phrases might include:

* "I'm making progress a little bit at a time."
* "I have figured out many new things before and I will again."
* "Look how much I've done already and how much progress I've already made."
* "I can finish this if I just take it one step at a time. I can go at my own pace."

Self-talk is a habit. As with most habits, it can take a little time and practice to change your current behavior pattern to a new one that sticks for you.

When it comes to changing our self-talk stream, quantity and consistency is key.

As with all patterns of thought, it can take a little time to change your self-talk habits. As Andrew Newberg and Mark Waldman, authors of the *Words Can Change Your Brain* blog, explain:

> When doctors and therapists teach patients to turn negative thoughts and worries into positive affirmations, the communication process improves and the patient regains self-control and confidence. But there's a problem: the brain barely responds to our positive words and thoughts.

The solution to this negativity bias? "We must repetitiously and consciously generate as many positive thoughts as we can" (Newberg and Waldman 2012).

In the beginning, changing your self-talk can often feel like you're arguing with yourself, back and forth, endlessly. You might think something like "I'll never get it done!" and then argue back to yourself, "I can do it in small steps!" and then answer back, "You'll never finish and you're going to mess it all up!" to which you might answer, "No, I won't! It will be fine!" And so on, and so on.

Be **persistent and consistent**, even when it feels very uncomfortable. Eventually, your **self-talk pattern** will start to shift, and then it won't feel like it's so much "work" to manage. It will become a habit that sticks for you. You might find, when this happens, that you're also naturally starting to procrastinate a whole lot less, too. You can remember it like this:

CRITICAL SELF-TALK + STRESS = PROCRASTINATION

Change the way you're talking to yourself, and you'll change how much stress you're feeling, and this can change your tendency to procrastinate as well.

Psychology researchers at Carnegie Mellon University in Pittsburgh found that stressed-out participants who were told to give themselves self-praise affirmations during a problem-solving test did better overall than those who didn't. The researchers concluded that "self-affirmations can buffer the effects of chronic stress on actual problem-solving" (Creswell *et al.* 2013).

If you're struggling to shift your self-talk in a more encouraging direction, you can start by introducing a more **neutral form of self-talk** first.

What does neutral self-talk sound like? This is a way of talking to ourselves that doesn't tip us over, emotionally.

Here's an example of **neutral self-talk:**

Task: **Building a new bookshelf.** Neutral self-talk:

* "These instructions are quite complicated, but if I just go really slow and take it one step at a time, I will figure it out eventually."
* "I can always look online to see if there are any videos I can watch about it that might be more helpful."

Notice how, in this rendition, we're not criticizing ourselves, we're not exaggerating the task, and we're not doubting ourselves. On the other hand, we're also not denying that this task is challenging to do.

We're simply acknowledging *what is*. That's all. Just **what is.**

Start with just stating the facts. From there, from that neutral place, more **encouraging self-talk** can start to grow.

We can lean more into **kindness** with the way we're talking to ourselves each day. We can show ourselves more **self-compassion** when we're doing challenging new things.

Kindness motivates us to move,

criticism stops us in our tracks.

So, as we move forward in this book, let's practice being a little kinder towards ourselves, as much as possible.

The support factor

Regulating our stress levels and **monitoring our daily self-talk** are two factors that can help to address chronic procrastination. **The third factor** that can help us start to move forward is **finding accountability and support.** Accountability means that instead of working towards a goal all on your own, you are actively seeking outside help to track your progress forward.

Sometimes, as kids, we may have felt like we had to frequently find our own unique workarounds for getting things done. Perhaps we were criticized a lot, and perhaps people didn't always understand our approach to things, so we learned to isolate ourselves and work through tasks on our own. I find this is especially true with high-achieving clients with ADHD. On the outside, they seem to accomplish so many impressive things almost effortlessly, but on the inside, they often feel like they are struggling to do it all on their own, without a lot of help or outside support, from a really stressed-out headspace. This feeling of "having to figure it out all on their own" can frequently result in overwhelm, exhaustion, and procrastination.

Finding accountability and support may be the piece we are missing to get ourselves un-stuck and moving forward again. In a study on accountability undertaken at the American Society of Training and Development, 65% of participants completed their goal if they committed to doing it by telling a partner. When participants had a regular accountability appointment with this partner, 95% of them completed their goal (Oppong 2017).

When we have to tell someone about what we are working on, we're bringing the goal from the intangible world of our imagination to the tangible world of actionable steps. Although this transition may seem overwhelming at first, it's often the fastest way out of the procrastination fog for most people. Now that another human is clearly involved as a witness, we can't just hide away in our own heads with our own ideas, wandering around in our own fog any more.

We have someone along with us for the journey now, and this can often help us stay more motivated and focused on what we need to do. It can also help us to remember to stay balanced, to take breaks, and to bring our stress down more deliberately. In other words, it can help us monitor our pace of reaching our goals in a healthier way.

As we start to navigate our way out of the procrastination fog, we want to avoid adding any further layers of harsh criticism onto our journey, whether it's coming from ourselves or from outside sources. So, it's important to find someone who is positive, kind, and encouraging to witness your goal progress from now on.

Schedule a consistent weekly check-in with a friend who can act as your "goal sponsor." If you can, support them back as they work on goals at the same time. You're not looking for someone to give you advice in this scenario; you're simply looking for someone who can witness your weekly progress from a supportive and encouraging place. It's helpful if you can also provide this to them as well, so that both of you can feel motivated to continue consistent check-ins over time.

If you can't find someone who fits this description right now, try to find an encouraging therapist or coach who specializes in goals, to help you navigate your way out of the fog. You can even bring the worksheets in this book to your sessions, as a way to investigate your own internal processes in greater depth together.

Some people may find the accountability they need by using **"body doubling."** Body doubling is when you enlist someone to be "present" while you are working on a task. Typically, a person will sit quietly with you while you work on a task for a limited period of time. While this is still a relatively new practice for adults with ADHD, it's theorized that it works well for some people because of the subtle social pressure that it provides. Knowing someone is present while you're doing a task may help you narrow your focus down for that specific period of time.

Another way to find accountability is through **weekly tracking** in a journal. This is a way to hold yourself accountable for every step you're taking by writing down all of the small steps you take each week in a short bullet-note list. As you make your way through this book, you will find worksheets ahead that will explain easy methods to start tracking your steps each week.

When we can see our own progress written out before us in a visual map, it's much easier to stay consistently motivated about moving forward. In this way, we can begin to prove to our own brain that we *are* making progress, and if our brain wants to argue back that we *aren't*, we now have written proof otherwise.

Tracking helps us find *irrefutable evidence* that we are moving ourselves forward consistently, a little bit at a time. Small steps add up!

And with each tiny step, we can practice feeling the feelings we want to feel along the way.

3

Types of Procrastination

Now that we've covered the **three factors** that will help us stay balanced and grounded in our journey, we can start to explore the **different sizes and forms of procrastination.**

Procrastination happens to everyone. It pops up in big ways and little ways throughout everyday life. Even the super high-achievers you may admire on social media are probably procrastinating *something* right now. Let's normalize that for a minute. Everyone procrastinates something!

Micro- and macro-procrastinations

A lot of people aren't just procrastinating big things right now, such as changing jobs, finishing huge projects, moving to new cities, or completing degrees. I call these **macro-procrastinations** and they tend to happen in big doses across longer stretches of time.

In sessions with clients, I've often noticed that **micro-procrastinations** tend to cause just as much as anxiety and stress as **macro-procrastinations** do, and often lead to more regular self-criticism.

Micro-procrastinations are smaller everyday things that we tend to put off doing, such as returning emails, scheduling appointments, doing laundry, organizing rooms, exercising, flossing teeth, starting a new habit, practicing self-care, finishing reading a book, remembering to drink enough water, or calling/texting people back. Perhaps, even as you're reading this, you're thinking, "Oh yeah. That's me. I avoid all those things!"

You are not alone. I want you to understand this, so you can stop beating yourself up about it. A lot of people are avoiding doing everyday tasks like flossing their teeth, scheduling appointments, starting new habits, or returning that email right now.

And sometimes, people will feel *more* guilt and shame about **micro-procrastinations** than they do about **macro-procrastinations** because they feel like "Everyone else can do these daily things; what's wrong with me?" or "Why are these little things so hard for me to do each week?"

Our **executive functions** can influence whether or not we are prone to chronically procrastinate. Executive functioning is a set of brain functions related to working memory: our ability to sustain focus, prioritize tasks, follow directions, and regulate our emotions and stress levels. In a 2021 study, researchers found that students who reported difficulties with executive functioning also had high levels of procrastination (Rinaldi, Roper, and Mehm 2021).

ADHD is often associated with procrastination and difficulties with executive functioning. For people who have an ADHD diagnosis, or suspect they might have ADHD (which would include having five or more ADHD symptoms for longer than six months, which can be assessed by a doctor or a psychiatrist), common executive functioning issues can include trouble controlling impulses or emotions, problems with organizing and planning, trouble focusing on tasks and sustaining attention, losing objects and forgetting things, and trouble prioritizing tasks.

The good news is, we can improve our executive functioning skills just by working on them consistently. And one way to do that is by completing the worksheets and exercises in this book.

Take your time with these tools. You'll be strengthening those executive functions with each page you fill out. You'll be figuring out new ways to catch procrastination, one page at a time.

Helpful and unhelpful procrastinations

Procrastination can be a confusing subject for people to explore because there are times when "putting things off on purpose" can be healthy for us to do, especially when it comes to prioritizing certain tasks over others, to clear the way for our own focus.

Let's call this **"helpful task prioritization"** instead of "procrastination." In this case, you're making some tasks a higher time priority than others intentionally, which can often be very helpful to do.

An example of helpful task prioritization: I have to file my taxes *by Friday*, so I delay doing my chores on Thursday so I can make time to focus on adding up all my expenses. I am clearing the path for myself to focus by prioritizing doing taxes over doing chores that day.

When we're thinking about when the best time will be for us to focus on something, and we're arranging tasks in a way that helps us, this would be an example of helpful task prioritization vs. unhelpful procrastination.

To cram or not to cram?

When it comes to procrastination, "cramming" often confuses people as to whether or not it's a helpful type of procrastination. Many people tend to say things like "I usually wait to cram it all in right before the deadline and it often works out well for me!"

This is usually a once-in-a-while thing to do, like waiting until the last hour to write a college essay and somehow pulling it off by racing through it at a manic stress-inducing speed. However, if used too much or too often, cramming can lead to burnout and exhaustion.

As a productivity approach, cramming tends to create more chaos than it solves. Consider that there may be easier ways to motivate yourself more regularly (and with more kindness) than giving yourself *even more* stress to manage.

As we work through this book, let's work on bringing our stress down, instead of raising it even higher.

Real breaks vs. Procrasti-breaks

Taking regular breaks is very beneficial for our brains, and it's important that we take them to reduce our stress. During a break where we *actively* bring down our stress levels, we are giving ourselves *more* neural energy for future problem-solving. This is often why after you take a "real break," during which you actually let your brain relax, you can sometimes look at the same project you've been working on with "fresh eyes" and know exactly what to do next. This kind of sudden clarity experienced after taking a healthy break can feel like real magic. This is what regular downtime can do for our brains.

Our brains need downtime to process information, store memories, and generate new ideas. According to Ferris Jabr: "Downtime replenishes the brain's stores of attention and motivation, encourages productivity and creativity, and is essential to both achieve our highest levels of performance and simply form stable memories in everyday life" (Jabr 2013).

It's essential that we get enough downtime each week, to replenish our own ability to focus on tasks ahead and to restore our general energy levels.

However, how does taking a healthy break from a task we're working on sometimes turn into a sneaky procrastination where we can't get ourselves back on track again? Has this ever happened to you before? When we cross this line over into **task avoidance**, I call this a **"Procrasti-break."** It simply means that procrastination caught you off-guard somewhere along the line during a break from doing the task.

You can often tell if you are starting to procrastinate by the way it's making you feel emotionally. There are usually **early internal cues** that you can start to notice when procrastination is setting in. For example, if you're taking a long break from a project or task, and you're starting to feel **a lot** of resistance about returning to the task again, you can ask yourself: "Is this a sneaky form of procrastination starting to set in?"

If the answer is yes, then don't worry, there are worksheets in this book designed to help you navigate your way out of it. By completing your journey through this book, you will get to know all the **different types of procrastination** (including the super sneaky ones like **Procrasti-breaks**) and you'll learn how to call them all out when you see them.

Recognizing the signs

At this point in the book, it might be helpful to ask yourself: "Is the procrastination I'm doing right now helpful or unhelpful?"

You will know the answer by how you *feel*.

Here are some possible ways to tell if it's a **helpful form of procrastination:**

* You haven't been procrastinating for very long.
* You have a clear plan for starting the task.
* While you may not necessarily be excited or thrilled by the task ahead, you are also not feeling too "weird" or "shut down" or "in denial" about doing the task altogether.
* Your form of "delaying doing something" includes a plan for taking things one step at a time and getting ready to move forward.
* You are in motion and not feeling stuck.
* You have an intention, a plan, and you believe in your own ability to complete the task.
* You feel okay with how you're approaching the task.

Here's an **example** of a helpful form of procrastination:

I had to turn in final grades for a class I am teaching by Friday. But on Monday, I delayed grading the final exams so I could focus on clearing out some business requests that were due. I was **prioritizing tasks** I needed to do so I wouldn't feel too overwhelmed later. I knew that by the end of the week, I would catch up with the grading of exams. And on Friday, I sat down and graded the exams until I was fully done. In other words, **I had a plan, an intention, and I believed in my own follow-through of this task at a clear point in the future.** And at some point this week, I prioritized doing the task and I completed it as planned.

It was procrastination with a purpose done on purpose.

Now, let's take this example and make it an **unhelpful form of procrastination:**

On Monday, I delayed grading exams and got distracted by an endless stream of business emails I had to reply to, which took me a few hours to do. Then, instead of going back to the grading, I decided to run a bunch of errands because I just couldn't look at the exams. Friday came, and I beat myself up all weekend because I didn't complete the grading by the deadline. Now, it's Tuesday, the office is asking where the grades are, and I'm stressed out and can't get started. Also, I feel like I'm in trouble, and I'm feeling pretty bad about myself.

This is why we want to **catch procrastination** at its onset, before the deeper and more intense feelings of **insecurity and shame** really start to set in for us. This requires us to start to identify what the early **internal cues of procrastination** look like to our own particular brains.

Here are some examples of early internal cues of unhelpful procrastinations:

* You feel a lot of internal resistance when you think about doing the task.
* You can't relax or focus on other things because it's bothering you that much.
* You don't have a plan for starting and you don't want to make one.
* The avoidance of getting started has been going on a while.
* You feel "weird" or "overwhelmed" or "shut down" when you start to think about taking the next step.

* You might be feeling this way about many tasks you need to do and not just one.
* You have a chronic habit of feeling this way about many things, and your to-do list is piling up.
* You are feeling very stuck.
* You are beating yourself up a lot about doing this task, and it's making you feel worse.
* You do not have a clear plan, a clear intention, a clear timeline, and you're not feeling very confident about your ability to follow through.
* You don't feel okay with how you're approaching the task.

These are just possible examples of how to begin to **read your own internal cues** about your own procrastination. As everyone's brain works differently, this book requires you to start to get really honest about **what you are doing when you're doing it** when it comes to procrastination.

Going forward, we're going to become more aware of the unhelpful forms of procrastination as they appear. You're going to get really good at **catching your own procrastination before it catches you.**

The Procrastination Clouds

Now that we have a general understanding of procrastination and how it can affect our brains and moods, how can we start to become **proactive procrastination catchers**? Let's remember our formula for catching procrastination:

THIS GUIDEBOOK CAN HELP YOU:

- **CALL IT OUT** (Notice the warning signs of procrastination clouds and call them out)
- **PLAN IT OUT** (Label the specific type of procrastination and pick a strategy forward)
- **TAKE ACTION** (Make a clear decision to act and take the first step out of there)

To move forward, we now need to learn **how to catch procrastination** so that we can call it out quicker. Let's learn to catch all the shapes and sizes of **procrastination formations** before we get too lost for too long in the haze.

Procrastinations can either be **visible forms of procrastination** (above the surface, easier to catch) or **subtle forms of procrastination** (under the surface, much harder to catch).

Visible forms of procrastination

Think of **visible procrastination formations** as big and fluffy cumulus clouds that loom overhead in the sky, making them easier to spot coming your way.

Task avoidance procrastination is when you clearly are avoiding a task you don't want to do, and it's usually obvious to you (and those around you). You may even admit to yourself, "I'm avoiding this task I need to do that's due on Monday. It's Sunday and I haven't even started." In this way, it's one of the easier forms of procrastination to catch.

Sometimes, we're avoiding a task we have to do because it "doesn't feel fun to do." Other times, it's because "it's too complicated" or "it feels too big and intimidating" to begin. You may even notice that your talk about the task leans towards negative exaggerations: "This task is a nightmare!" or "I'd rather [fill in something bad] than do [task]." In order to catch this type of procrastination, all we have to do is listen to how we're talking about the task in front of us.

When you're avoiding a task and it feels obvious to you that you're avoiding it, you can start calling it out as it appears: "This is **task avoidance procrastination**."

Time management procrastination is when your procrastination is related to **time** in some way. Either you didn't plan enough time out to do the task because you **underestimated** how long something would take, or you didn't map out your schedule in a way that allowed you to do the work effectively.

Sometimes, **time management issues** may arise from **hyperfocusing** on a piece of the task you needed to do (getting too zoomed in on what you're doing and losing track of time altogether), which is often caused by **time blindness** (losing track of our own internal ticking clock and ability to track time).

Time blindness and **hyperfocus** are often associated with common ADHD symptoms. According to Dr. Michael Manos:

> Everybody has time blindness at times, we all get caught up in something and get "in the zone." Some people with ADHD, though, are more prone to having difficulty being able to judge how long something will take to do or to lose track of time. (Cleveland Clinic 2023)

Time management issues also sometimes come from having **inaccurate time estimations** of what we're about to do (e.g., "This report will take half an hour to write" when in reality, it will take *three hours* to write). Once you catch yourself doing this **form of procrastination,** you can then complete worksheets in this book that will help you map out your time more effectively.

Prioritization procrastination is when you feel stuck because you don't know which task to do first or which step to take next in order to move forward. This is called **task prioritization**, and it's linked to our ability to make a decision about what's the most important thing to do next.

On the outside, this type of procrastination often looks like jumping around from one task to the next, without a clear plan or purpose. You're just trying to put out every single fire as it appears and handling way too many things all at once...except for the *one thing* that you are avoiding handling altogether.

For example, instead of doing the work that you've planned out to do, you start vacuuming your living-room rug. Instead of making that dentist appointment, you start organizing the files on your laptop because they're distracting you. Or, on the way to the library to work on your paper that's due tomorrow, you wind up going to the mall to look for a new pair of shoes. In that particular moment, buying shoes somehow got flagged by your brain as more important than finishing your paper, even though your paper's deadline is tomorrow.

If this happens to you, and you spot it, call it out for what it is: **"task prioritization procrastination."**

HALF-WAY DRIFT

Have you ever drifted off half-way through a task and then found that you've lost your way and can't finish it? Sometimes, we complete part of a project, and our brain marks the project as "done" too quickly, and as a result, we never finish the final piece. We get so excited that we are so close to the finish line that we forget, momentarily, that there are still steps left for us to complete.

In other words, we start the celebration party waaaaay too early.

Why is this a **visible form of procrastination?** It's typically easier to catch because it's probably fairly obvious to you (and possibly others around you) that you only have a little bit left to do. Watching someone get stuck in this kind of procrastination can be especially frustrating to loved ones, because they often just want to celebrate with you, and may be eagerly waiting at the finish line, with champagne in hand. And it's equally frustrating on the inside of this procrastination fog, as it tends to make us feel an intense sense of guilt and shame as a result.

Here are some examples from clients:

"I filled out the forms to renew my passport for an upcoming vacation, and I was so proud of myself for finishing the forms because I don't like forms, but then I forgot to send them in! I never even put them in the envelope after I printed them. Now, I have missed the deadline and I'm embarrassed that I didn't complete the task."

"I wrote about 75% of my novel. I took a break because I needed one. The break stretched on for a year (I kept putting off starting again). Now, I have no idea where I was going with the chapter I left off on, and I feel like I don't even want to write it any more. I don't even remember what I was doing with the plot. I am mad at myself for getting lost half-way."

"I bought a rowing machine to get more exercise. I never put it together. It's still sitting in the box in my living room. It's now been there for a month and my girlfriend is getting grumpy."

In our excitement to be done with certain parts of a task, it's easy to sometimes forget the smaller parts of a task that are still remaining (e.g., mailing in your passport forms or sending the email in your drafts folder). We need to remember that there are smaller pieces we still need to do in order to be "fully done" with the task.

For this reason, it can be helpful to outline what "half done" vs. "fully done" is for yourself on paper. For example:

HALF DONE	FULLY DONE
Finish writing last chapter of novel	Send novel to my publisher before due date
Order rowing machine	Put it together and put it in the spare room

Don't worry, this happens to everyone sometimes. We've all ordered stuff before and then pretended the unopened box wasn't sitting in the middle of the hallway for a week or two. There are all sorts of variations of this, and many of us do them frequently, throughout everyday life.

Look for the "half" vs. "fully" done markers in your own life and start to get more sensitive to noticing them as they're happening to you. So, the next time you catch yourself doing the half-way drift:

* **CALL IT OUT** ("Half-way drift")
* **PLAN IT OUT** (Define what "fully done" is to yourself)
* **TAKE ACTION** (Set a deadline to do the next step and plan the first step forward)

And then, after you complete the final parts of the task, celebrate all you want, because you will really and truly be done.

In other words, let's get to "fully done" before we throw the celebration party.

Subtle forms of procrastination

Now that we've reviewed the visible forms of procrastination, let's move on to ones that are much sneakier in nature. These **subtle forms of procrastination** are trickier to spot and much harder to catch as they're happening to you. Think of subtle procrastinations as those nimbostratus clouds that cover the sky in a dense gray layer and aren't as easy to see coming.

In my book *The Ultimate Time Management Toolkit*, I talk about how everyday distractions will sometimes turn into **"time sinkholes."** This is where you accidentally derail yourself from making progress on a task or goal by going down a **time sinkhole** with something that you're using to distract yourself (e.g., social media, video games, show binges, doom-scrolling, etc.).

Sometimes, we think the **time sinkhole** we're going down is "productive" or "helpful." On the outside, it could look like we're "working on things," but these things might not actually be helping us move forward at all; they might just be "side quests" that take us away from our main mission.

People often tell themselves they are using **time sinkholes**, such as scrolling through their phones, as a way to "take a breather" or to "de-stress" when, in reality, the **time sinkholes** may be stressing them out *way* more than they think. Have you ever felt depressed or stressed out after hours of scrolling through your phone? And then have you felt even more depressed/stressed out when you realized that the hours you set aside to work on a specific task have now all vanished into thin air as a result?

A study done at the University of Pennsylvania found that when participants used Snapchat, Facebook, and Instagram for over 30 minutes a day, they felt more isolated and depressed than those who didn't use the apps, and when these participants decreased their usage of these apps to under 30 minutes a day, they felt less lonely overall and it generally "improved their sense of wellbeing" (Hunt *et al.* 2018).

This is why **time sinkholes** are a sneakier form of procrastination, because you might not always realize that you're slipping into them on a daily basis.

Many people spend big chunks of their time each week lost in time sinkholes, without even knowing it.

Time spent in **time sinkholes** definitely adds up, and it's also sometimes a way that we subconsciously procrastinate doing something.

PERFECTIONISM

Perfectionism is a particularly harsh form of **self-criticism** where you tell yourself you need to be "perfect" or "do something perfectly" or "find the perfect tools/gears/app/class" before you can begin. This is one very quick way to get yourself feeling *perfectly* stuck, because what you're essentially telling your brain is that the task ahead is impossible, as it's impossible for anyone to do anything "perfectly."

A recent study published in the journal *Psychiatry Research* showed that perfectionism was the most common self-reported "cognitive distortion" among adults with ADHD:

> Results indicated a significant, positive correlation between self-reported cognitive distortions and ADHD. Responses to individual items on the measure of cognitive distortions were tabulated to identify the prevalence of specific cognitive distortion categories, with Perfectionism emerging as the most frequently endorsed. (Strohmeier *et al.* 2016)

So, if you have ADHD, you may also be prone to perfectionism, and it could even be the reason you are procrastinating something right now.

Instead of defaulting to perfectionism, we can learn to go a little **gentler and kinder** towards ourselves, loosen up, and expand our idea of what "making progress" means to us. If you allow other people to make mistakes and go at their own pace, why wouldn't these same rules apply to you? Don't make up different unfair rules that you have to endure. Make them the same gentle rules you have for other people. You deserve your own support and encouragement, too.

Waiting for motivation is a very **sneaky and subtle form of procrastination** because, on the outside, it may look like someone is waiting around "for motivation to kick in." It may even look like they have a plan in place and are just "waiting for the right moment" to start—only the "perfect moment" never arrives. This is what happened to me when I got lost in my own procrastination fog for five years. I kept waiting for the motivation to zap me with one giant burst of energy so I could move forward, but it never did. So, I never started.

Motivation doesn't usually come in like a lightning bolt while we are standing still, waiting indefinitely, not moving forward.

Motivation tends to zap moving objects, not stagnant ones. You can remember it like this:

Motivation finds us after we start moving.

It's counterintuitive, but it's often the case. Once we start moving ourselves forward, our focus and attention kicks in, which makes us suddenly feel more motivated to keep going.

In other words, you won't really feel very motivated when you're inert. The *longer* you stand still, the *less* motivated you will feel. You have to take a step first, and then another, and then the motivation can find you.

Analysis paralysis often looks like "overthinking" or "over-researching"

something before you can begin. When this type of sneaky procrastination sets in, you might find yourself going into **"research time sinkholes"** that make you feel even more lost and confused, instead of feeling more motivated to begin.

Here are a few examples of **analysis paralysis procrastination** from clients:

"I told myself I would start recording music when I found the perfect pair of headphones. Only, I kept finding different reviews of headphones online, I kept getting stuck reading them all, and I never picked one to buy, so I never got started on my music project."

"I kept hunting for an app that would help me organize my calendar so I would stop procrastinating. I downloaded three different apps, kept trying them out, and none of them worked. In the end, I wasted a few weeks trying out productivity apps, and the whole time I didn't realize I was procrastinating."

"I was researching stuff for a book but I kept buying new books to read for research. Now there is a stack of books on the coffee table. I haven't read any of them, and I haven't written my book either. I'm really overwhelmed even looking at them."

Often, this happens to people at the starting line of their goals, because the road ahead looks too intimidating to start down. It's easy to let ourselves think we're "getting ready" for a while, when we're actually subconsciously delaying getting started. After all, some mental preparation and research can be helpful to do when we don't know how to proceed yet.

However, if the "getting ready" stage is stretching on way too long, you might want to ask yourself whether or not a sneakier **form of procrastination** has caught you off-guard. You'll know by the **internal cues** you're feeling about starting the project and the amount of avoidance you're feeling about taking the first step.

To get out of the **analysis paralysis loop**, we need to give ourselves a

deadline to begin, and then we need to figure out what the next logical small step forward is.

We don't need to have every piece figured out ahead of time. We can take a few steps and figure it out as we go. More information will become available to us with every step we take. We can always correct course as we receive more data, but we won't know what that data is until we actually start moving ourselves forward first. Trust in your ability to figure it out as you go. You've done it before with other things, and you'll do it again and again, too.

If you're waiting for things to be "perfect," what you're really telling your brain is you're waiting for things to be "impossible."

Remember, you can't move forward if your brain thinks it's impossible.

Instead, tell your brain it's *possible*, and now your brain can help get you to where you want to go.

In this very sneaky form of subtle procrastination called self-protection, we try to "protect ourselves" by not moving forward. We use this type of procrastination as a big shield. However, there are certain times when this particular shield isn't helping us to grow; it's helping us to stay stuck in our own fear instead.

SELF-PROTECTION FROM TIME COMMITMENTS

We protect ourselves from different things. Sometimes, it's from a time commitment (e.g., "I can't commit to working on that project every Friday for the rest of the year!") because our time estimate of how long we think the task will take to do hasn't been fully examined yet.

When we're feeling stressed out, there's often a tendency to make negatively exaggerated time estimations of how long tasks will take us to complete. These exaggerated estimations are often based on how we're *feeling* rather than on actual *facts*.

Stress causes our brains to grossly exaggerate how much time things will actually take us to do.

Reality is often so very different than what we are imaging inside our brains. Often, what we're imagining is a harsh and extreme version of something that probably won't even come true.

How often have you experienced some version of this in your own life?

Just this past week, a client said to me, "I finally filled out the form I've been avoiding for six months."

"How long did it take you to do?" I asked him.

"It took me ten minutes. I have been torturing myself about it for six months! I really don't know why I thought it would be so hard. All that time, I thought it was going to take days fill it out. But in reality, it only took a few minutes!"

When has your own stress tricked you into thinking something would take forever when in reality it only took a few minutes to do?

QUICK JOURNALING EXERCISE

Write about a recent example of when your brain inaccurately exaggerated how long something would take you to do.

. . . .
. . . .
. . . .
. . . .
. . . .

If you catch yourself procrastinating because of "exaggerated time estimates" you may have formed, call it out:

* **CALL IT OUT** ("Self-protection procrastination—time estimates")
* **PLAN IT OUT** (Figure out how much time it will actually take on paper)
* **TAKE ACTION** (After figuring out an accurate time estimate, find a slot of time during the weekly schedule to take the first step)

Call it out, plan it out, and take action. And when it comes to making time estimations, let's focus on *facts* over *feelings* from now on.

SELF-PROTECTION FROM FAILURE, JUDGMENT, OR SUCCESS

Sometimes, we might be using **self-protection procrastination** as a way to protect ourselves from what other people will think about us if we fail, or even if we succeed. You can see how this becomes a no-win situation that we've created for ourselves. If we fail, people will judge us; if we succeed, people will judge us. If we take any step forward, people will judge us. In this imaginary nightmarish scenario, there is absolutely no way anything good can happen. So, why even begin at all?

As a result, we "shut down the show," so to speak, before anyone has a chance to see us perform. Don't pull that curtain down before you've even taken that first step on stage. Give yourself a fair chance to try something new.

While most people *logically* understand that they aren't really being watched and judged all the time by others, somehow they don't *emotionally* believe it to be true. They may say something like "Yeah, I know everyone is too busy with their own lives to notice what I'm doing," but underneath it, they still feel like "Somehow I know they're going to judge me anyway."

Does this resonate a little with you? It can be helpful to think of it this way:

Often, our fear of "judging eyes" is really just about our own judgment of ourselves.

The harsher we are being on a daily basis towards ourselves, the more we tend to expect that others will also judge us harshly, too.

The way we're talking to ourselves affects what we're hearing from those around us. If we're being overly critical towards ourselves, we tend to *notice* signs of criticism from other people more easily. If we're encouraging ourselves a lot of the time, we tend to *hear* encouragement from others more easily. In other words:

What we have trained ourselves to hear, we will hear.

And, as we can't control other people, let's address part we can control— **how we're talking to ourselves.** Tell yourself you can do it, that you're going to figure it out. Tell yourself you can go your own pace. Tell yourself it's going to be okay and you're learning as you go. It's also helpful to remember:

Sometimes the uncomfortable parts of growth are less uncomfortable than staying stuck.

New things tend to cause anxiety and stress in many people. And the first few steps of new things are especially anxiety-inducing sometimes. But staying stuck across the years is also very anxiety-inducing as well. And once you realize that, it gives you more courage to take that first tiny step into the unknown.

The more you can go **gentler and kinder** in your self-talk, the more you'll be able to ride out that initial wave of uncomfortable feelings when it arrives. And then you can get to the other side of it, where newfound confidence and strength is waiting for you.

Reading the signs

Now that we're getting more savvy at identifying the different forms of procrastination, let's review our procrastination catcher's formula:

THIS GUIDEBOOK CAN HELP YOU:

- **CALL IT OUT** (Notice the warning signs of procrastination clouds and call them out)

- **PLAN IT OUT** (Label the specific type of procrastination and pick a strategy forward)

- **TAKE ACTION** (Make a clear decision to act and take the first step out of there)

The internal cues

So, how do we go about *taking action*? If you can start to catch the **internal procrastination cues** when they appear, you can then take the appropriate action and get yourself out of the procrastination fog a whole lot faster. This is really what **pro-active procrastination** catching is all about.

Just as you can step outside sometimes and get a sense that rain is on the horizon from that crisp smell in the air or that mist upon your nose, you'll now be able to sense when the procrastination clouds are forming overhead.

So, what are the **procrastination warning signs** that you're starting to procrastinate? Here are some examples from clients:

"I start binge-watching Netflix shows but I can't really focus on watching them and they don't feel fun. Even so, I keep clicking on the next episode anyway, even though I feel bad about it."

"I let papers stay in a pile on my desk but I don't look at them. My warning sign is piles of paper!"

"I don't open my mail. The pile of mail gets bigger and bigger."

"When there is work I am avoiding doing, I buy clothes online. I start to shop way too much online and make lots of questionable purchases."

"I get distracted cleaning the house instead of finishing what I need to do. I get a lot of cleaning done and I don't do anything else. Avoidance-cleaning, I call it."

"I can't focus on what's happening in the moment because I am too distracted by my own non-stop thoughts of the task I am avoiding doing."

"Instead of focusing on the task, I start calling or texting people and getting distracted in other people's dramas. I start looking for people to distract me."

"I spend way too much time scrolling on my phone and I start to lose track of time a lot. But I feel guilty the whole time I'm doing it."

"I get grumpier; I get short-tempered and snap at people around me for no reason."

"My ADHD symptoms will flare up when I start avoiding doing something. I forget lots of little things and I start to overbook my schedule. I think sometimes I get busier on purpose to avoid doing the thing I don't want to do."

"I go to great lengths to physically avoid my home office. I stay out of the house a lot. I see lots of friends, I run errands. I notice I don't want to be home a lot because that's where my computer is and my desk is and it reminds me of the work. I don't want to be in my office."

Do any of these sound familiar to you? Let's discover what yours are.

QUICK JOURNALING EXERCISE

Write out a bullet list of three to five signs that you are starting to procrastinate. What do you think you tend to do? What would other people say that you do when you are starting to procrastinate?

1. . . . .

2. . . . .

3. . . . .

4. . . . .

5. . . . .

So, now, when you see those papers piling up on your desk, when you start impulse shopping online, or when you catch yourself avoiding your own desk for days at a time, you can call it out when you see it. You might say something like this: **"This might be an internal cue that I am starting to procrastinate."**

Learn to catch the cues before the procrastination catches you.

And then you can decide to get yourself un-stuck by making a decision to get out of the fog altogether. It can be helpful to remember:

* Tell yourself you have a plan, and the fog will start to lift.
* Set a clear date to start your plan, and the fog will begin to disperse.
* Take that first step forward, and the fog will disappear.

Getting Started

Why do we procrastinate?

People procrastinate for a wide range of reasons. These reasons vary from project to project, from person to person, and they can often change depending on how stressed out we are, how much energy we have, how we're feeling about ourselves, or how we're feeling about what we have to do in that particular moment.

Sometimes our reasons for procrastinating can run really deep, in which case it may be helpful to take the time to explore these things with a therapist, as they may be connected to past experiences, ADHD, trauma, depression, anxiety, or other issues.

Other times, our reasons for procrastinating may not run deep at all. We may just have a pattern of thought going on that simply isn't working out for us. And sometimes that pattern of thought just needs a *tiny amount* of shifting to get us moving again.

So, let's start making that first **tiny shift**, right now, and see what happens. Are you ready?

The first tiny shift

We live in busy times, and most of us have busy lives where we are trying to juggle avalanches of information, communication, and stimulation coming at us each day. It's altogether too easy to put off things you want to do, with the idea that you'll "do it tomorrow" or "get started in a month or two."

But then time slips away from us, and then we're still thinking about starting that project or goal years later, while still not moving ourselves anywhere closer to where we want to go.

"I'll get started tomorrow," you might keep saying, as tomorrow turns into another tomorrow and another one.

Instead, let's consider going a little easier on our **"tomorrow selves"** by getting really honest with ourselves...today.

Tomorrow-You won't be able do all of the tasks and projects you are pushing forward into the future unless **Today-You** starts moving forward in small steps in that general direction.

Tomorrow-You will not have any more motivation than **Today-You** does.

If anything, **Tomorrow-You** will have *less* motivation, because pushing tasks into the future tends to make those tasks feel even *more* overwhelming and *more* stressful to complete when you actually start doing them.

So, let's make things easier for **Today-You**, right now.

Today-You: You can go at your own pace. Take as much time as you need to learn these new skills and tools that will help you long after you finish this book. You're already showing a lot of courage by reading this far and learning new ideas that can help you take that first small step forward.

Give yourself some credit right now, and give yourself credit each step of the way. Let's cheer ourselves on from this point forward, instead of beating ourselves up any more.

Take it one skill at a time, one page at a time, one step at a time.

When you want to give up, it can be helpful to remember:

Do something today that helps your future self in some way.

You've got this!

Now, let's pick up that pen and get started.

How to use the worksheets in this book

There are two different ways to do the worksheets in this book:

1. **You can pick the "Choose Your Own Adventure" path through the worksheets.** I've provided an interactive way to navigate through the worksheets ahead, if you want to take it. At the **Starting Line,** select what you would like to work on, and then choose a path to follow by following the prompts on the bottom of the worksheets, until you cross the **Finish Line.** At any point, if you find yourself on a page you've already done or if you want to jump ahead to a different page, you can **fast-track to the Finish Line** by going to **The Procrastination Signs** worksheet (p.171).

→ To begin this path, go to page 67 (**The Starting Line**).

2. **Alternatively, you can work your way straight through the book,** starting at the **Worksheet Checklist.** Simply go through the worksheets, one after another, until you get to **The Finish Line.**

→ To begin this path, go to page 71 (**Worksheet Checklist**).

Note: The accompanying PDFs can be downloaded from https://library. jkp.com/redeem using the code YZXZYPH

A NOTE

The workbook is not intended as a replacement for psychotherapy or medical advice. It is a book of creative tools to help you figure out new ways to approach areas in your life where you're feeling stuck. When these worksheets are done in conjunction with therapy, they can really boost your motivation and momentum.

Remember, **you actually have to write the worksheets out, in order for them to work for you.** So, pick up that pen and let's go!

You can do it!

I'll see you at **The Finish Line** to celebrate.

PART 2

BEGIN YOUR JOURNEY

THE STARTING LINE

Welcome to the start of your journey!

List out a few things in each column that you are **currently procrastinating** doing. As we learned in Chapter 3, **macro-procrastinations** are big tasks, goals, or projects that you are procrastinating, typically over a longer stretch of time; **micro-procrastinations** are everyday habits or smaller tasks you are procrastinating, usually over a shorter period of time.

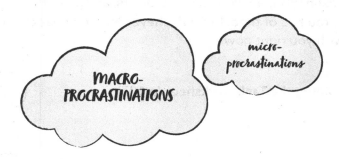

Macro (big things):

1. . . . .

2. . . . .

3. . . . .

Micro (small things):

1. . . . .

2. . . . .

3. . . . .

Now pick ONE THING ONLY and CIRCLE IT NOW.

→ If your task is on the **Macro** list, go to the **Macro-procrastinations** section below

→ If your task is on the **Micro** list, go to the **Micro-procrastinations** section below

→ If you don't know what to pick, go to **What Kind of Procrastination Is It?** worksheet (p.73)

Macro-procrastinations

Macro-procrastinations are large tasks, projects, and goals that we're avoiding doing over stretches of time. Pick whichever "procrastination cloud" resonates most with you right now:

→ Go to **Avoiding the Task** worksheet (p.107)

→ Go to **Time Management Procrastination** worksheet (p.78)

→ Go to **Task Prioritization** worksheet (p.84)

→ Go to **Half-Way Drift** worksheet (p.150)

→ Go to **Getting Distracted** worksheet (p.153)

→ Go to **Roots of Perfectionism** worksheet (p.137)

→ Go to **Motivating Self-Talk** worksheet (p.130)

→ Go to **Avoiding the Task** worksheet (p.107)

→ Go to **Making Decisions** worksheet (p.113)

I'm not sure which procrastination to pick...

→ Go to **What Kind of Procrastination Is It?** worksheet (p.73)

Micro-procrastinations

You've found yourself on this page because you would like to work on a **micro-procrastination**. Micro-procrastinations are smaller tasks, projects, or habits that we're avoiding doing, and they can often cause us to feel just as

much guilt, shame, and anxiety as **macro-procrastinations**, which are bigger things we're avoiding.

Micro-procrastinations can be things like small projects or organizational projects we need to complete, or they can be everyday things we are avoiding doing regularly, such as chores or errands. They can also be habits we are trying to start but just can't get ourselves to begin or do consistently.

To figure out where you want to go next, choose one of the following:

I want to work on a smaller task, project or goal that I've been procrastinating...

→ Go to **First Steps: Micro-Procrastinations** worksheet (p.93)

I want to work on a habit that I've been procrastinating doing...

→ Go to **Working on Habits** worksheet (p.91)

I am not sure if this is a micro- or macro-procrastination...

→ Go to **What Kind of Procrastination Is It?** Worksheet (p.73)

WORKSHEET CHECKLIST

You've found yourself on this page because you want to work through all of the worksheets in the book and you want to do them in order. That's great—you're really going to become an active procrastination catcher after you complete all of the worksheets ahead.

Here is a checklist of all the worksheets in this book. Feel free to go through and check all the ones you complete. I'll see you at the end of the book to celebrate all the things you've learned!

- ☐ What Kind of Procrastination Is It? (p.73)
- ☐ Time Management Procrastination (p.78)
- ☐ Time Frames for Goals (p.82)
- ☐ Task Prioritization (p.84)
- ☐ Time Mapping (p.85)
- ☐ First Steps: Goals and Projects (p.88)
- ☐ Working on Habits (p.91)
- ☐ First Steps: Micro-Procrastinations (p.93)
- ☐ Activation Energy (p.96)
- ☐ Planning Rewards (p.102)
- ☐ Setting Intentions (p.105)
- ☐ Avoiding the Task (p.107)
- ☐ Organizing the Steps (p.110)
- ☐ Making Decisions (p.113)
- ☐ Extreme Thinking Glasses (p.116)
- ☐ The Avoidance Onion (p.122)

☐ Roots of Procrastination (p.125)

☐ What I Can Tell Myself (p.127)

☐ Motivating Self-Talk (p.130)

☐ Different Rules (p.132)

☐ Roots of Perfectionism (p.137)

☐ Facts vs. Feelings (p.139)

☐ The Encouragement List (p.144)

☐ The Finish Line Picture (p.146)

☐ Future-You Letter (p.148)

☐ Half-Way Drift (p.150)

☐ Getting Distracted (p.153)

☐ Where Does Time Go? (p.154)

☐ Time Blocking (p.156)

☐ Time Tracking (p.161)

☐ The Procrastination Signs (p.171)

☐ The Stress Signs (p.173)

☐ Self-Talk Review (p.175)

☐ Accountability Review (p.177)

☐ The Procrastination Round-Up (p.179)

☆

What Kind of Procrastination Is It?

You are stuck trying to figure out what kind of procrastination you have. You would like to know: "Why am I stuck here in procrastination?"

Let's write about it and see what happens.

Answer the question below:

Where am I getting stuck with this task/project/goal? List all the ways:

. . . .

. . . .

. . . .

. . . .

. . . .

. . . .

. . . .

. . . .

. . . .

. . . .

. . . .

. . . .

. . . .

Looking at all the reasons I've written above, which sticks out to me the most as the main reason I'm procrastinating right now? Circle the **main reason** above.

→ Great job! Now, go to the **next page**.

☆

Which procrastination is it?

Circle the quote that best matches what you wrote down on the previous page.

→ Go to **Time Management Procrastination** worksheet (p.78)

→ Go to **Getting Distracted** worksheet (p.153)

→ Go to **Task Prioritization** worksheet (p.84)

☆

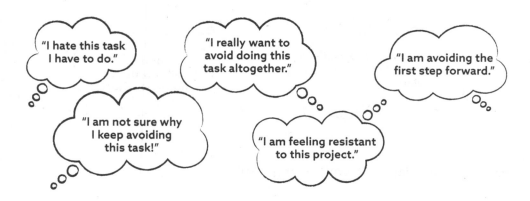

→ Go to **Avoiding the Task** worksheet (p.107)

→ Go to **Roots of Perfectionism** worksheet (p.137)

→ Go to **Motivating Self-Talk** worksheet (p.130)

→ Go to **Half-Way Drift** worksheet (p.150)

→ Go to **Setting Intentions** worksheet (p.105)

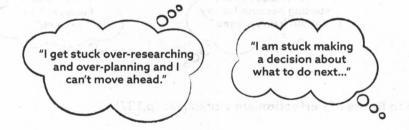

→ Go to **Making Decisions** worksheet (p.113)

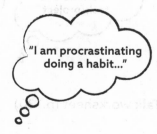

→ Go to **Working on Habits** worksheet (p.91)

☆

"I need help talking to myself in an encouraging way about finishing this task."

"I need to find ways to talk myself into doing this task."

"I am being overly critical towards myself about how I'm doing this task."

→ Go to **Motivating Self-Talk** worksheet (p.130)

☆

Time Management Procrastination

You have discovered that you are lost in **"Time Management Issues"** procrastination fog.

Let's try to figure out what types of **Time Management Issues** you may be experiencing, so that we can get your goal-ship back on course again.

Read through all the descriptions and try to **find the one that resonates with what you are experiencing right now** and then **jump to the corresponding page**.

Waited Too Long (and Now It's Due)

Form: **Visible Procrastination**

In this classic form of procrastination, you find that you have waited too long to start your task/project, and now it's due, and you are completely overwhelmed. You are so overwhelmed, in fact, that instead of beginning, it's easier to just use "magical thinking" and pretend that you have more time than you actually do. This type of "magical thinking" will not actually change how many hours there are left on the clock. And, unfortunately, we have now run out of actual hours! So, the time has come to move ourselves forward and that time is now.

Let's start by admitting this to ourselves and accepting it:

"The time has come for me to take the first step towards my goal. I am starting today. I am going to feel so much better after the first few steps are over. I can feel proud of myself for taking this first step forward."

Now that we've gotten ourselves to admit that we're starting right now, how do we proceed with this big overwhelming thing we have to do (that is now due)?

Let's break that big thing down and figure out what the first step forward is.

→ Go to **Time Mapping** worksheet (p.85)

Time Commitment Problems

Form: **Subtle Procrastination**

In this subtle form of procrastination, we are avoiding taking on a task or project because it feels like the task will take "too much time" or "too much energy" or "too much of a time commitment" to move forward with it. It's a subtle form of procrastination, because in our heads, we may still be considering the options, but on the outside, we are not moving forward... at all.

These "self-protective" feelings are sometimes good to listen to as they may be prompting us to set healthier time boundaries for ourselves with things we may not want to really do. Other times we use this form of procrastination as a vague way to **never get started** on things we **really do want to do**. So, the first step is to figure out if you really want to do this thing. After that, we can move on to figuring out how much **actual time** it's going to take you to do it!

→ Go to **Setting Intentions** worksheet (p.105)

Too Busy to Do It

Form: **Visible Procrastination**

☆

In this more visible form of procrastination, you know why you want to do the task; you just can't find any time in your current schedule to do it. It's a visible procrastination because you're probably very visibly busy right now and your calendar is most likely stacked full of stuff. Perhaps, you've over-booked other things, or said yes to too many other activities, and now you're feeling "crushed for time."

The first step will be to find out how much **actual time** you will need to do your task, and then we can figure out where to position it in your schedule where your mental energy will be best.

→ Go to **Time Mapping** worksheet (p.85)

No Set Deadline

Form: **Subtle Procrastination**

This is a very sneaky form of procrastination because we keep waiting to set some deadline for ourselves, and then...we just never set one!

Only, we have a vague feeling that we're working on setting the deadline for ourselves, so it gives us a false sense of movement. Or, even more common, we have already set many deadlines for ourselves, blown right past them, and then told ourselves we need to set even "better deadlines" for this to work. However, then we just ignore the "better deadlines"! I call this a **deadline-setting loop**.

In the famous words of author Douglas Adams (2002), "I love deadlines. I love the sound they make as they go whooshing by." If this is you, and you need some kind of deadline for yourself that you will stick to:

→ Go to **Time Frames for Goals** worksheet (p.82)

☆

Can't Find Consistent Weekly Time

Form: **Visible Procrastination**

Perhaps you were making progress toward your goal, and then, for whatever reason, you got stuck somewhere along the way? And now you think the reason might be that you can't find consistent enough time to keep moving yourself forward? In this case, you need either (a) a time map of how to proceed or (b) motivation to start moving again. Pick one:

→ For **"I need to map out the next steps,"** go to
   Time Mapping worksheet (p.85)

→ For **"I need more motivation before I begin,"** go
   to **Setting Intentions** worksheet (p.105)

→ **Not sure?** Go to **Time Frames for Goals** worksheet (next page)

☆

Time Frames for Goals

Before you begin your steps forward, it's important to check in to make sure that your time frame to complete your goal/task/project is **realistic and reasonable**. What does this mean?

Let's find out. Write out **your goal** and **when you expect to complete it**:

MY GOAL: . . . .

. . . .

GOAL DEADLINE : . . . .

Now, I want you to **read what you wrote above** to yourself out loud.

When you read this to yourself, did you wince or cringe a little? Did you feel **resistance** of any kind? Did you hear your own words and think, "Yikes!" or "Why on Earth am I doing this to myself?!"

Did your own words make you feel like giving up altogether?

If you had this reaction just now, the problem might be that your **deadline** is not **reasonable or realistic**. If it sounded reasonable, you wouldn't be feeling the cringe-worthy resistance you're currently feeling right now and you probably wouldn't be procrastinating.

When we make our deadline too *intense*, our brain responds with *intense* emotions, and this slows down any forward motion altogether. We need to bring the stress down by stretching the deadline out to fit into a more reasonable and manageable-sounding time frame.

So, let's lower our stress a little, before we go any further.

Now, I want to encourage you to look at your goal through a **"kinder lens,"** one that allows you to have enough time to do each step without all the unnecessary stress. One that feels compassionate, instead of stressful and harsh.

Let's be kinder to our brains so that our brains can move us forward with this. When in doubt, **double the length of time for your deadline**, if at all possible.

And so, let's try this exercise one more time from the top, looking through a **kinder lens** this time.

Write out your goal again:

MY GOAL: . . . .

. . . .

MY NEW (KINDER) GOAL DEADLINE: . . . .

And let's just do the same test. **Read the goal and deadline out to yourself. Listen to your own words.**

Did that make you feel like "Oh, that sounds a little better"? If not, keep stretching that deadline out until it gets into a more reasonable range for you. When it sounds better and gives you that little lift of relief, you're ready to move to the next step!

→ **Let's keep going.** Go to **Time Mapping** worksheet (p.85)

☆

Task Prioritization

You've found yourself on this page because you would like help prioritizing what step to take next. Often when we're experiencing **task prioritization procrastination**, we're having a hard time deciding what to focus our attention on in an effective way.

Before we can move forward with figuring that out, choose from one of the following:

I am procrastinating a big goal, project or task...

→ Go to **Time Mapping** worksheet (next page)

I am procrastinating a smaller goal, project or task...

→ Go to **First Steps: Micro-Procrastinations** worksheet (p.93)

I am procrastinating starting or doing a habit...

→ Go to **Working on Habits** worksheet (p.91)

☆

Time Mapping

You've found your way to this page because you're avoiding a big project, task, or goal. We will need to break that big thing down until we find the first step forward. Let's grab a pen and start figuring out all the different steps of your goal.

Disclaimer: Do not attempt to do this worksheet in your head; you will need to write it out for the worksheet to work for you.

TASK:. . . . .

Write out a reasonable deadline: . . . .

QUICK CHECK-IN

- Is this deadline I am setting for myself **reasonable and realistic?**

- Do I need to stretch this timeline out **even more** to show myself more compassion?

→ Go to **Time Frames for Goals** worksheet (p.82) to work on this, if you think you need more help.

Now, let's work backwards from our deadline. When will the project/task be **HALF DONE** by? (divide the amount of time between now and your final deadline):

The **HALF-DEADLINE** of this project will be (write down the date):

. . . .

After you find your half-deadline, walk yourself backwards to where you are now, at the starting line. Then ask yourself: What is the very **FIRST STEP** forward?

The **FIRST STEP** will be done by (write down the date):

. . . .

Great job. You're almost there!

Our timeline now looks like this:

> **FINAL DEADLINE:** . . . .
>
> **HALF DONE BY:** . . . .
>
> **FIRST STEP START DATE:** . . . .

Good job! We're getting closer to starting now. Let's keep breaking it down...

Steps Breakdown

Now that you have mapped out your deadline, write out the **small goal steps** you will take to get to your final goal.

STEPS TO GOAL:	END DATE:
▶	. . . .
▶	. . . .
▶	. . . .
▶	. . . .
▶	. . . .
▶	. . . .
▶	. . . .
▶	. . . .

☆

Looking at your step breakdown, do you now have a better idea of what weekly steps you will take to complete your goal?

Are you ready to take the first step forward?

Yes! I am ready to take that first step forward now! Let's go...

→ Go to **First Steps: Goals and Projects** worksheet (next page)

I still need help feeling motivated to begin...

→ Go to **Setting Intentions** worksheet (p.105)

I am ready to plug the steps into my schedule...

→ Go to **Organizing the Steps** worksheet (p.110)

☆

First Steps: Goals and Projects

You've found your way to this page because you've just broken down your big project or goal into smaller steps! If you haven't done that yet, go to the **Time Mapping** worksheet (p.85). If you're working on breaking down a habit or smaller task into steps, skip to the **Working on Habits** worksheet (p.91).

We're going to continue to break that goal down until you feel motivated to move forward, by naming our first step, setting a first step deadline, and then giving ourselves a tiny **mental nudge** to complete it.

To do this exercise, list the task you've been avoiding. Now, set a **realistic time frame** for completing your task. If you need help with this, go to page 82. Figure out what the very **first step forward** is, and then write out a **first step deadline**.

After this, your **first step prep** is a **visual cue** that you give yourself to move forward with your **first step**. It's a cue to tell your brain you're ready to get ready. For example, if your first step is taking a daily walk, your **visual cue** might be to put your sneakers by the front door so that the next morning, you will see your shoes and remember to take the walk.

Making things easier on your brain is the quickest way to overcome any kind of procrastination.

Examples from clients:

TASK: *Complete a painting.*

REALISTIC TIME FRAME: *6 months.*

HALF DONE BY: *3 months from now.*

FIRST STEP: *Buy the color paints I need.*

DATE OF FIRST STEP: *In two weeks.*

☆

FIRST STEP PREP: *Put out my blank canvas on an easel in the living room so I can tell myself I am serious about doing this painting.*

TASK: *Self-publish my children's book.*

REALISTIC TIME FRAME: *1 year.*

HALF DONE BY: *6 months from now.*

FIRST STEP: *Write out a story outline in my notebook.*

DATE OF FIRST STEP: *Tomorrow.*

FIRST STEP PREP: *Put my notebook in the middle of the dining-room table so I remember to do it in the morning after breakfast.*

TASK: *Complete a certification course online for work.*

REALISTIC TIME FRAME: *3 months.*

HALF DONE BY: *End of this month.*

FIRST STEP: *Sign up for the course.*

DATE OF FIRST STEP: *Monday.*

FIRST STEP PREP: *Make a list of possible places to take the course, write it on a post-it, and stick it on my computer so tomorrow I remember to research them.*

☆

Now it's your turn:

TASK: . . . .

. . . .

REALISTIC TIME FRAME: . . . .

HALF DONE BY: . . . .

FIRST STEP: . . . .

. . . .

DATE OF FIRST STEP: . . . .

FIRST STEP PREP: . . . .

. . . .

. . . .

Great job! You've given yourself that first mental nudge to move. Now, let's cement things further by providing your brain with a motivation boost!

Good work! Let's keep going...

→ Go to **Activation Energy** worksheet (p.96)

☆

Working on Habits

You've found yourself on this page because you want to work on a habit you've been avoiding. Let's answer the following questions before we move on to figuring out the next step forward.

Write out the answers to the questions below:

Why am I avoiding doing this habit?

. . . .

. . . .

. . . .

What are the parts of the habit that I'm feeling the most resistance to doing?

. . . .

. . . .

. . . .

What are some practical ways I can make this habit easier on my brain?

. . . .

. . . .

. . . .

Example 1: *I can make the habit of taking a daily walk easier on myself by planning to do it every day after dinner, listening to my favorite podcast while I walk, and by setting a reminder on my phone to take the walk.*

Example 2: *For the habit of remembering to take my multivitamin, I can put the bottle out on the kitchen counter, I can take it at the same time each morning with my coffee, I can tell my partner I've done it afterward so I have accountability.*

☆

Example 3: *Instead of telling myself I have to do yoga every single day, I can do yoga once a week to start and build from there. I can tell myself once a week is better than none at all, and I can track my weekly progress on a calendar by giving myself a sticker each time I do it!*

Now it's your turn. List out 1–3 ways you can make this habit easier on your brain:

1. . . . .

2. . . . .

3. . . . .

List 1–3 reasons why you should start this habit now instead of later:

1. . . . .

2. . . . .

3. . . . .

What will you tell yourself when you want to procrastinate this habit from now on? Write out 1–3 things you can tell yourself:

1. . . . .

2. . . . .

3. . . . .

Great job! Let's continue...

→ Go to **First steps: Micro-Procrastinations** worksheet (next page)

☆

First Steps: Micro-Procrastinations

You've found your way to this page because you've been avoiding a smaller type of task or starting a new habit. This is an everyday type of thing that's been nagging at you, a small project you need to move forward on, or a habit you would like to begin.

What we need to do is to break the task or habit down into the tiniest first step forward, so that your brain will feel like it's easy and manageable to do.

First, write down the task you've been avoiding:

. . . .

. . . .

Now, set a realistic time frame for completing your task:

. . . .

If you need help with giving yourself a reasonable time frame and deadline, go to the **Time Frames for Goals** worksheet (p.82) to work on setting one for yourself.

Now, figure out what the very first step forward is, and then write down a first step deadline:

. . . .

After this, your **first step prep** is the **mental nudge** you give yourself to move forward with your **first step**. It's a visual cue to tell your brain you're ready to go. For example, if your first step is taking a daily walk, your **first step prep** might be to put your sneakers by the front door so that the next morning, you will see your shoes and remember to take the walk.

☆

Examples from clients:

TASK: *Cleaning up leaves in the backyard.*

REALISTIC TIME FRAME: *One month.*

FIRST STEP: *Clear out half the yard.*

DATE OF FIRST STEP: *In two weeks.*

FIRST STEP PREP: *Buy a new rake today and put it by the backdoor so I remember to start.*

TASK: *Flossing my teeth regularly.*

REALISTIC TIME FRAME: *At least 2 or 3 times a week.*

FIRST STEP: *Put the floss picks in a clear jar on top of the counter so I see them each morning.*

DATE OF FIRST STEP: *By tonight.*

FIRST STEP PREP: *Buy the floss picks and new clear jar on the way home from work today.*

TASK: *Turn in my receipts from my work trip.*

REALISTIC TIME FRAME: *By Thursday.*

FIRST STEP: *Find all the receipts that are somewhere in my luggage.*

DATE OF FIRST STEP: *Monday.*

FIRST STEP PREP: *Pull out my luggage from the closet today and open it up.*

☆

Now it's your turn:

TASK: . . . .

. . . .

REALISTIC TIME FRAME: . . . .

FIRST STEP: . . . .

. . . .

DATE OF FIRST STEP: . . . .

FIRST STEP PREP: . . . .

. . . .

Great job! You've given yourself that first mental nudge to move. Now, let's cement things further by providing your brain with a motivation boost!

→ Go to **Activation Energy** worksheet (next page)

☆

Activation Energy

You've found yourself on this page because you've already planned your **first step prep** (if you haven't, go to page 88), or you've just completed the **Half-Way Drift** worksheet (p.150), and now you're feeling like you're almost ready to start moving forward.

Starting is often the hardest part of any task, so let's ramp up your **activation energy** so you feel ready to take those few first steps forward.

Activation energy is a term used in chemistry to define the minimum effort needed to get a chemical reaction. In psychology, we use **activation energy** to mean the minimum level of effort needed to move ourselves forward. This is a way to prepare ourselves mentally, and to ramp up our motivation.

We can accomplish this in different ways. Provided here are some different **activation energy strategies** that you might want to try using to spark your motivation. While reading through the descriptions, please check off the ones that you would like to try using in the future.

☐ Timers

A popular timer method that helps many people getting started on tasks is called the Pomodoro Method. Setting a timer on your phone or a kitchen timer for 25 minutes, you would work on the first step of your task until the timer beeps. Then you would take a break to relax, or move on to other tasks you need to do. If you wanted to start working on the chosen task again, you would set the timer for another round of 25 minutes, and then stop again when the timer beeps. You can play around with the length of time. Some people like to do 15 minutes instead of 25 minutes. Just keep the time limit consistent for each burst.

Why this works for some people: Working in short and predictable bursts helps many people narrow their focus down on what they need to do. It makes working on a task seem more manageable because they know they'll only have to do it for 25 minutes, and this is a length of time that doesn't seem that overwhelming to a lot of people. It also can help with time blindness, as a way to keep us from going into hyperfocus for too long with a task.

Why it doesn't work for some people: Some people don't like the pressure of a timer ticking down and spend the whole time worried that they are running out of time. Others find the beeping of the timer too jarring and too disruptive to their flow. If this is the case for you, try out some different ideas below.

☐ The Music Timer

For those who don't respond well to the Pomodoro Method, you might want to try using a music playlist as a timer instead. Using this technique, you would make a playlist ahead of time and use it every time you are working on a specific task. I've been using this music timer technique for many years to help me to write in limited time frames. I have a "writing playlist" which mostly consists of classical music that I play every time I sit down to write. It's become pleasantly predictable for me as I enjoy hearing music while I write, but you can pick out any type of music that works best for your brain to use to focus. Choosing the same music each time can be helpful to do, as it becomes a way we can gauge how long we're working on something, based on the length of the playlist.

Why this works for some people: Some people find it less intrusive to listen to a music playlist that runs out after a certain amount of time, rather than hearing a timer beep at them. And if we're selecting music that feels energetic and uplifting, it can have mood benefits, too. Studies have shown that music affects our feelings of motivation, our moods, and our energy levels, which is why so many people use music playlists to do workouts at the gym (Cherry 2022). Just as we might use a playlist to exercise to, we can also use a playlist to exercise our brains more intentionally.

Why this doesn't work for some people: Some people may require complete quiet to work, and they might get easily distracted by music, as music often brings up past memories and other emotions. Also, some people will get

☆

lost in a time sinkhole trying to pick what music to use, and they won't get started on the task. For this particular tool to work for you, I would suggest making your playlist the day before you intend to use it, so you don't get too distracted by choosing songs while working on a task.

☐ Brain Warm-Up

Here is a creative tool that I have used with many clients over the years. The Brain Warm-Up involves picking a short activity that "warms up your brain" to focus. The activity should be less than a half hour and should not be something that will stress you out or make you lose your focus altogether. For example, one client uses crossword puzzles as a way to "warm up" his focus to be able to write. He does a crossword puzzle for 15 minutes and then goes straight into writing his book. Another client uses journaling as a warm-up activity for preparing to read through his work emails. Some even use going for a walk as a way to "warm up" their brain to focus. During their walk, they think about the task they will start doing when they get back, to "prep" their brain to do it. Think about an activity that might get your brain "in the mood" to focus and try it out!

Why this works for some people: This tool works best if you think, "I'm using this activity as a way to warm-up my brain," and then you would go right into doing the task after you're feeling warmed up. It can be a way to "trick" our brains into focusing on the task we're avoiding doing, by getting our brains to do a short task that feels more engaging to do first.

Why this doesn't work for some people: Sometimes, people get too distracted with their Brain Warm-Up and they forget to work on the task they're avoiding. In this case, the Brain Warm-Up becomes a time sinkhole instead. So, if you're going to try out this tool, make sure you're clear to yourself about working on the task you're procrastinating *right after* the warm-up ends.

☐ The Stopwatch Method

I developed something I call the Stopwatch Method after I realized other types of timers were not working for certain clients. This is the *opposite* approach to a clock clicking down in time. In this case, it's a stopwatch you click when you start the task. There is no set limit. You just see how long you can go on the task before you stop the stopwatch. The trick here is that you must record how much time you did in a notebook, even if you only did the task for three seconds. Then you track your data across a week and add up how much time you did altogether.

Why this works for some people: Some people feel motivated by seeing how long they can do a task without any set limit. They like the idea that over the course of the week, they can prove to themselves they did something by adding up the data. It can also sometimes take off the pressure of having to do a set amount of time. For them, a stopwatch gives them more freedom than a timer does. Jotting down how much time they completed also can "gamify" focusing for some people.

Why this doesn't work for some people: Some people don't like the idea of a "running clock" as it creates a low level of pressure. Others will forget to track their data, and so they won't feel motivated as a result. Seeing the collected data over a length of time is an essential piece of why this technique motivates us to keep going with the task, so it's the part you will need to remember to do for this tool to work for you.

☐ Mental Rehearsal

Using this visualization technique, take a few minutes to picture yourself doing the very first step of the task. Then walk yourself *past* the point where you've completed it and to the point where you're feeling better about the whole task, emotionally. How does it feel to have completed the first step of your task? Are you proud? Relieved? Happy? Try to evoke those emotions as you're imagining yourself doing it.

☆

Why this works for some people: When we visualize doing the first step, we are activating the motor cortex areas of our brain, so that our brain feels like we are actually doing what we're imagining. The more you imagine yourself doing it, the more it feels like you've actually done it, so, in theory, the less resistance we will have to doing it in reality.

Why this doesn't work for some people: Some people get stuck on imagining only the stressful parts of the task, which makes them want to procrastinate starting the task even more. In order for this exercise to work, you have to walk your imagination past the stressful parts of taking the first step to the part where you feel more confident and relieved that it's over. You have to imagine the emotions you want to feel instead of the ones you don't want to feel.

☐ Visual Cues

Using visual cues can be very helpful to remind us to do something. Figure out what visual cues might work for you and your specific task, habit, or project. I use a weekly post-it note which I put on my desk lamp so I have to look at it every time I sit at my computer. I write out the three things I want to remember to do each week, including things I have caught myself procrastinating. Other people use alerts on their phone or specific objects that remind them of the task which they place somewhere visible that they can't easily ignore. What might work as a visual cue for you and your task?

Why this works for some people: If you can find a visual cue that grabs your attention, you will be more likely to do the task, goal, or habit. For example, if I wanted to remember to drink more water throughout the day, I might leave a few water bottles out in visible places to remind me to take them with me. Or if I wanted to remind myself to take a walk, I would put my sneakers by the front door. Or if I wanted to work on painting something, I might put my paint brushes out in the middle of the dining-room table. *Remember: If we can see it, we are more likely to do it.*

Why this doesn't work for some people: Visual cues only work if they are actively grabbing your brain's attention. However, our brains can start to ignore cues sometimes (e.g., we start to not see the post-it we've placed on our desk lamp or we step over the shoes we've put by the door), and then the visual cue has stopped working for us. This tool requires us to notice when these cues stop working and to change them regularly for ourselves, to grab our brain's attention again.

☐ The 15-Minute Rule

Using this strategy, you would tell yourself something like, "I can do this task for 15 minutes at a time." At some point in the week, you would just do 15 minutes of the task. And at the end of the week, you would check in with yourself to make sure you did the minimum of 15 minutes.

Why this works for some people: Most people feel like they can do 15 minutes of almost anything. It's easy for most people to find a spare 15 minutes during a whole week's worth of time to do something. Often, this tool gets people over the "starting line stuck-point," and then they find that they're doing way more than 15 minutes of the task and they're not counting any more. They don't need to use the tool for very long because they've now tricked their brain into doing more than the required amount of time.

Why this doesn't work for some people: Some people might find themselves procrastinating doing the first 15 minutes over and over again, and they just can't get themselves past the starting line stuck-point in this way. If this is the case for you, check out the next worksheet on rewards, as this might be an easier tactic that feels more fun for you to do.

Which of these activation energy tools resonated the most with you? Which did you have the **least resistance** to trying out this week?

And now, let's plan some rewards as a way to get you moving forward...

→ Go to **Planning Rewards** worksheet (next page)

☆

Planning Rewards

You've found yourself here because you have mapped out the steps of your goal, and now we get to plan some fun rewards for completing steps along the way.

Often, the hardest part of a new thing we're taking on is the first step forward. It's the one we typically will resist the most, because it feels so uncomfortable and uncertain (and often frustrating). And as we know, motivation tends to find us *after* we start moving forward.

So, how about we plan a very small reward for completing the first step? When it comes to rewards, it's important that you pick something that is easy for you to do, just for you, on your own. You can always add **bonus rewards** later that involve other people. However, for now, we're practicing celebrating our successes on our own, in an easy way. So, think of something small and easy to do, something that is healthy and makes you happy, and that you can use as a small treat to get you through each step.

Sometimes, people will use **delayed gratification** as a reward. For instance, they will save the episode of their favorite TV show to watch *after* they've done the first step. You can use this, or figure out another type of small reward that sounds fun to your brain. It's helpful if you can save the *most* satisfying reward for last, while planning mini-rewards for important steps along the way.

Explain the **part of the task** and the **corresponding reward** you will give yourself for doing that specific piece of it. Here are examples from clients. The first two examples are for rewarding goals, and the last one is for rewarding a habit:

TASK: *Organizing kitchen.*

REWARD FOR FIRST STEP: *I will take myself out to my favorite coffee shop for an iced latte after I throw out all the old stuff in the first cabinet.*

☆

REWARD FOR HALF-WAY DONE: *I will buy new tea towels at my favorite store after I've cleaned out three of the six cabinets.*

REWARD FOR TASK COMPLETION: *I will save watching all my favorite Netflix show episodes and binge-watch them when I am done with cleaning out the six cabinets.*

TASK: *Finish filling out my staff evaluations for everyone on my team.*

REWARD FOR FIRST STEP: *I will take a nice walk on the beach after I open up the evaluation forms and look at what I have to do.*

REWARD FOR HALF-WAY DONE: *I will order my favorite Italian take-out when I am done with 4 of the evaluations.*

REWARD FOR TASK COMPLETION: *I will treat myself to a day at the local botanical garden when I am done with all 8 evaluations.*

HABIT: *Going for a walk three times a week as a habit (goal: make it to two months).*

REWARD FOR FIRST STEP: *I will end my very first walk at my favorite juice store and buy myself a fresh juice.*

REWARD FOR HALF-WAY DONE: *After one month of doing walks three times a week, I will treat myself to a massage.*

REWARD FOR TASK COMPLETION: *After two months of doing walks three times a week, I will treat myself to a day at the spa.*

Now it's your turn:

☆

TASK: . . . .

. . . .

REWARD FOR FIRST STEP: . . . .

. . . .

REWARD FOR HALF-WAY DONE: . . . .

. . . .

REWARD FOR TASK COMPLETION: . . . .

. . . .

HABIT: . . . .

. . . .

REWARD FOR FIRST STEP: . . . .

. . . .

REWARD FOR HALF-WAY DONE: . . . .

. . . .

REWARD FOR TASK COMPLETION: . . . .

. . . .

I am ready to plan out my schedule now...

→ Go to **Time Mapping** worksheet (p.85)

This is great! I want to feel even more motivated now...

→ Go to **Setting Intentions** worksheet (next page)

☆

Setting Intentions

(aka "Why do I want to do this thing?")

You've found your way here because you want to feel more motivated to take that first step forward with things. In order to begin, we need to get really clear about why we want to do this thing we're about to do. Ask yourself right now, "Why do I want to accomplish this thing I need to do?"

And now let yourself write out an answer below, listing out every possible reason you can think of:

Why do I want to accomplish this task/goal?

. . . .

. . . .

. . . .

. . . .

. . . .

. . . .

. . . .

. . . .

. . . .

Now, looking at what you've just written, let's simplify this down into **one clear sentence**. When we give ourselves a clearly stated reason to move forward, our brain can get on board with getting us there.

It all starts by telling yourself **exactly why** you want to do something.

Write out your intention in one simple sentence using the template provided below.

☆

For example:

- ▸ "My intention for completing this certificate is to learn a new skill, which will make me feel more confident at work."
- ▸ "My intention for completing this decoration project is to make my home office look nicer, which will make me feel more motivated."
- ▸ "My intention for completing my yoga class is to gain flexibility through stretching, which will make me feel healthier."
- ▸ "My intention for completing my research paper is to end the semester well, which will make me feel relieved."

Now it's your turn:

My intention for completing . . . .

. . . .

is to . . . .

. . . .

which will make me feel . . . .

. . . .

We've now told our brain how we want to feel afterwards. We've given ourselves a green light to go!

Are you starting to feel that motivation kick in yet? Let's keep going and see if we can boost it some more.

Let's work on understanding our own procrastination more...

→ Go to **The Avoidance Onion** worksheet (p.122)

I want to work on improving my self-talk...

→ Go to **Extreme Thinking Glasses** worksheet (p.116)

☆

Avoiding the Task

You've landed here because you're currently feeling a lot of **avoidance** about what you need to do. Typically, when people find themselves here, there's a lot of harsh self-talk going on about the task, such as "I hate this task!" or "I don't want to do it!" or "Every time I think about starting, I just don't want to do any part of it" or "I can't even look at it!"

Let's start to think about where this **internal resistance** is coming from regarding this specific task by doing a very short warm-up exercise.

We will start with something easy and quick, and then work our way down to discovering if there are any deeper **layers of avoidance** lurking underneath.

For this exercise, I want to you to separate out the task you're avoiding into **two columns of steps** you need to do to complete the task. Take your time to really think about the individual steps of the task for this exercise. And then you're going to have to **get really honest with yourself** about **which pieces feel the most stressful** for you to do. Don't worry if steps feel stressful or not—just write it all down.

After years of doing this exercise with many people, I can tell you that many small steps are hard for many people, no matter what the task is. You would be surprised at what people rate as "stressful" and what they rate as "easy" for themselves to do. It's often things you could never predict unless you asked them to complete this exercise! So, let's be kind to ourselves right now. By acknowledging that **parts of this task feel hard for us to do**, we're learning to show ourselves more **self-compassion**. This typically **reduces our resistance** to doing the task ahead.

Remember: Kindness motivates us to move, self-criticism stalls us out.

☆

Task—Two Columns

To begin this worksheet, write out the **most stressful steps of the task you need to do** in the left column, and then write out **least stressful steps** in the right column. Try to figure which piece of the task you are feeling the most resistance and stress about.

At the bottom, write a **conclusion** of something you learned from doing this exercise. After you reflect upon your conclusion, write **something kind** that you can tell yourself about finishing the task ahead.

For example:

Task: Filing a reimbursement form at work

Most stressful parts	**Least stressful parts**
Finding all my receipts	Sending it when it's done
Filling out the form online	Getting paid
Learning the new forms	Next time, I will know how to do it

Conclusion: *I don't like filling out forms because I don't think I'm good at them. However, once I learn the forms, I'm usually okay the next time. I think I don't like doing forms for the first time.*

What I can tell myself: *"If you just get through the hard part at the beginning, and then it will be easy afterward. You can do it!"*

Now it's your turn:

Task: . . . .

Most stressful parts	**Least stressful parts**
. . . .	. . . .
. . . .	. . . .
. . . .	. . . .

☆

Conclusion:. . . . .

. . . .

What I can tell myself: . . . .

. . . .

Making this list, did you start to feel the resistance lift a little for you?

Great job! Let's keep going with exploring why I am avoiding this task...

→ Go to **Organizing the Steps** worksheet (next page)

I am ready to break my big task/goal down into steps...

→ Go to **Time Frames for Goals** (p.82)

I could use help talking to myself in a kinder way...

→ Go to **Extreme Thinking Glasses** (p.116)

☆

Organizing the Steps

You've found yourself on this page because you want to get a better idea of how to organize the next steps forward. You may be stuck making a decision on what to do next, or you may feel overwhelmed thinking about a particular piece of what you have to do.

First, we need to discover what all the different steps are of the task in front of you. Then we can begin to organize the steps ahead by figuring out how stressful each of the steps is for you to do.

Be honest in your rating of how much stress you're feeling about each of the steps and feel the differences between them. This will keep you from procrastinating because you'll be acknowledging and accepting your feelings about each step.

Then we can assess how long each step will take you to do. For this part, it's very important that you give yourself **more than enough time** to do each step! When in doubt, give yourself double the time.

When you expect yourself to do every step instantly, it will only increase your stress, which will lead you to want to avoid doing it. Give yourself enough time for each step!

To begin:
Let's look at **all the steps** of the task you need to do. Any step you can think of, list it out in the first column. In the second column, **rate how stressful** that step of the task feels like for you to do (**low stress, mid-stress, high stress**), and then in the third column, write out a **realistic time estimate** of how long the step will take you to do. Make sure your time frame is reasonable and realistic. **When in doubt, plan for more time than you think, rather than less.**

Finally, add up your **total time estimates** of steps at the bottom. Then write out a **conclusion** about what you've learned underneath and think about a time you might be able to move forward with the steps that best suits your mental energy.

☆

Then **set a date** based on your own data to begin!

Note: It's important that you write this one out on the page instead of trying to do it all in your head.

Here are a couple of examples:

Task: *Finishing my employee evaluation report*

Steps	Stress level of step	Time estimate of step
Figure out how to log into new form online	Mid-level stress	30 minutes
Fill out self-evaluation	Mid-level stress	30 minutes
Submit to supervisor	Low-level stress	5 minutes

Total time: *approx. 1 hour*

Conclusion: *This evaluation will only take me around an hour (or less) to do.*

Set a date: *I have an hour on Friday morning at 9 am, I will start then.*

Task: *Organizing the kitchen cabinets*

Steps	Stress level of step	Time estimate of step
Clean out stuff from shelves	High-level stress	1–2 hours
Order new containers to sort things	Low-level stress	30 minutes
Put things in the new containers	Mid-level stress	1 hour

Total time: *approx. 3.5 hours*

Conclusion: *This kitchen organization project will take 3.5 hours. I can't do it all in one day without getting stressed out. I am going to break it up into two or three weekends and do an hour at a time. That way, I can relax in between the hard and stressful parts.*

☆

Set a date: *I can start the first chunk of this task on Saturday afternoon after lunch at 1 pm. After that, I will follow up the following two Saturdays to complete it.*

See how this exercise works? By **writing things out** and **getting honest with yourself** about what **the stressful steps are** of the task you need to do, you can enlist the logical side of your brain to help you form an easier plan to do the task ahead.

And then you can make the clear decision to begin!

Now it's your turn:

Task: . . . .

Steps	Stress level of step	Time estimate of step
. . . .	. . . .	. . . .
. . . .	. . . .	. . . .
. . . .	. . . .	. . . .

Total time: *approx.* . . . .

Conclusion: . . . .
. . . .
. . . .

Set a date: . . . .
. . . .

This is great! I am ready to plug the steps into my schedule now...

→ Go to **Time Blocking** worksheet (p.156)

I still need help focusing with distractions...

→ Go to **Getting Distracted** worksheet (p.153)

☆

Making Decisions

You have found yourself on this page because you're getting stuck in an **analysis paralysis procrastination**, and you need to figure out how to make a decision to start moving forward. Sometimes, we need to establish what the **"good enough zone"** is for starting the task, or else we might find ourselves lost in a "waiting for everything to be perfect" procrastination fog.

Examples of finding the **good enough zone** for a task:

"I don't need to wait until next year to sign up for the painting class. I can start painting a little at home first just for fun. I already have all the supplies, I just have to give myself a chance to play around with the paints. That would be a 'good enough' starting point."

"Instead of saying I have to go running every day each week, I can start by taking a daily short walk around the block on days where I get home from work earlier. That's a 'good enough zone' for me for now and I can change it later."

"Instead of thinking that I can't use the music software until I've watched the entire video tutorial collection, I can say that in one month I will start playing around with the basics of it for a half hour. A half hour at the end of the month is a 'good enough zone' to begin."

It can be helpful to remember that if you're getting stuck on making a decision, you can remind yourself that you can always adjust things in the future, as you go. You'll figure it out each step of the way as you're taking the next one forward. You don't have to everything mapped out "perfectly" before you begin. There is no way to know now, at the starting line, all that will be ahead and all that you'll need to learn.

In other words, the only way out is through!

There is no way to "future predict" all the problems, you'll have to just learn as you go. You've done this before with other things you've learned, and you'll

☆

do it again with this task as well. Sometimes, it's just about remembering that you have done it before and telling yourself you will do it again.

Let's do a **quick exercise** to see where you're getting stuck on your task.

Where are you getting stuck with moving forward on this task?

. . . .
. . . .
. . . .
. . . .

Why do you think you are getting stuck here?

. . . .
. . . .
. . . .
. . . .

What would be a "good enough zone" for beginning this task? (e.g., "Instead of waiting to buy the perfect microphone to record my podcast, I can start with something I can afford and upgrade it later.")

. . . .
. . . .
. . . .
. . . .

What would you like to tell yourself about taking the next step?

. . . .
. . . .
. . . .
. . . .

☆

What is a very small action you can take next?

. . . .

. . . .

Set a date to start:

. . . .

Okay, now write out your plan:

TASK: . . . .

. . . .

GOOD ENOUGH ZONE: . . . .

. . . .

SMALL ACTION I CAN TAKE NEXT: . . . .

. . . .

DATE TO START: . . . .

I would like to break this task down into steps so I can figure out what to do next...

→ Go to **Time Mapping** worksheet (p.85)

I want to find time to start doing this task now...

→ Go to **Organizing the Steps** worksheet (p.110)

Let's keep working on staying motivated...

→ Go to **Extreme Thinking Glasses** worksheet (next page)

☆

Extreme Thinking Glasses

Often when we're avoiding doing something, we get into an **"extreme think-ing"** mindset that doesn't help us move forward at all. **Extreme thinking** is like wearing a warped pair of glasses that distorts and exaggerates the world around us. And when we put on these **extreme thinking** glasses, it has a way of stalling our forward progress towards tasks and goals. You can think of it like this:

Put on the "extreme thinking glasses" and prepare to procrastinate.

For example, when you put on these **extreme thinking glasses**, the task you have to do is instantly the worst task ever (*in the history of all tasks ever done in all the world*):

▸ you're going to do a terrible job at it (*worse than anyone else ever has done before*)
▸ everyone will be so mad at all the mistakes you're about to make (*which will be bigger mistakes than anyone else has ever made in the history of all the world*)
▸ and you're going to feel completely awful about the whole process no matter what the outcome (*for ever and ever, endlessly into the eternal future of all time*).

See how absurdly *extreme* that all sounds when it's written out in front of you? But that's just a *tiny taste* of the types of daily extreme thoughts that many people tend to think about things they're avoiding doing!

When you think about the fact that we think thousands of thoughts each day, you can see how this kind of **extreme thought looping** might really start to get you down about things you need to do...and about your ability to do them.

Listen for these **extreme words** in your talk about tasks:

- Always
- Never
- Nightmare
- Awful
- All the time
- Worst ever
- Horrible
- Hate

These just might be subtle cues that you are wearing **extreme thinking glasses**.

Just to normalize this, we all wear these distorted "extreme thinking glasses" from time to time. And sometimes we don't even realize we're wearing them.

However, when we have the glasses on, we tend to accept that what we are seeing through them is "the truth." But these glasses aren't showing us **facts**; they're showing us a distorted view of what's actually in front of us, based upon how we are **feeling** in that particular moment.

That's the real problem with wearing these "extreme thinking glasses." You start to unconsciously accept this exaggerated perspective as **facts instead of feelings**.

And so it's helpful to start to look at what the facts actually are, to begin to separate things out for yourself, and to find your balance again.

So, let's practice looking for **"just the facts"** instead and compare this to our **extreme thinking** on things we need to do.

"Just the Facts" Exercise

In the space below, write out the **"extreme thinking"** version of the task you are avoiding, and then write out the **"just the facts"** version, where you simplify it down to the basic facts of the situation.

☆

When we do a "just the facts" rendition, we want to sound **as factual as possible**. So, try to include an **accurate approximation** of the time this task is actually going to take you to do. This will help give you a broader perspective on things, going forward.

Steps for this exercise:

▸ First, write out your **"extreme thinking"** rendition of your task.
▸ Then write out your **"just the facts"** version of your task with an **accurate time estimate** of how long it will take you to do.
▸ Now, write out a **conclusion** based upon what you gained from looking at the two statements.

Here are a few examples from clients:

Extreme thinking: *"This awful email is going to take me so much time to write and I'll never finish it by 6 pm!"*

Just the facts: *"I need to send this email about the new office procedures by 6 pm today. That means I have three hours left to write it."*

Conclusion: *"I have three hours to write this email and, generally, it only takes me a half hour to write a detailed email. It really only has to be two paragraphs long. I have more than enough time to write two paragraphs before 6 pm."*

Extreme thinking: *"I'm the worst ever at writing papers and this one has to be longer than any other paper we've done in class, and the history professor is so mean, I know he's going to hate what I write no matter what I do."*

Just the facts: *"I have a history paper that is due by Friday and it has to be at least five pages long. This paper will take about an hour per page to write. If I do two pages a night, I will finish by the deadline. This particular professor doesn't like it when papers are late, so as long as I turn it on time, that is what matters most."*

☆

Conclusion: *"If I write a few pages a night for the next few days, I can complete the paper by the deadline."*

Extreme thinking: *"I will never finish this laundry in time for our trip this weekend because work is so busy and I never have enough time when I come home. And I really hate laundry as it sucks up my entire evening when I want to do other things!"*

Just the facts: *"I have three loads of laundry that I need to do before Saturday because we're going on a trip then. Each load of laundry takes 45 minutes which means the three loads will take me about two and a half hours to do."*

Conclusion: *"Two and a half hours is about the length of watching a movie. Maybe I can do the laundry while we watch a movie at home on Friday night, which then won't require that much extra time to do, and I get to watch a movie. That way, we can pack the clean clothes in time for our trip Saturday afternoon."*

Extreme thinking: *"No matter how hard I try, I can't start the daily habit of taking a walk. I'll never do it. I have tried everything and failed to do this habit."*

Just the facts: *"A walk around the block takes ten minutes. A short ten-minute walk a few times a week is doable in my schedule."*

Conclusion: *"I have ten minutes each morning before work for a short walk. I don't have to do it every day, because doing it a few days is better than zero days. And I don't have to take a long walk. I can start with a short walk around the block to begin with, and see if I want to do longer walks on days when I have more time and energy."*

After reading that, hopefully you're now a little inspired to try it out for yourself. Remember you have to write these exercises out on paper in order for them to work for you.

Now it's your turn. Try it with **three things you've been avoiding doing**:

Extreme thinking: . . . .

. . . .

. . . .

Just the facts: . . . .

. . . .

. . . .

. . . .

Conclusion: . . . .

. . . .

. . . .

. . . .

Extreme thinking: . . . .

. . . .

. . . .

. . . .

Just the facts: . . . .

. . . .

. . . .

. . . .

Conclusion: . . . .

. . . .

. . . .

. . . .

☆

Extreme thinking: . . . .

. . . .

. . . .

. . . .

Just the facts: . . . .

. . . .

. . . .

. . . .

Conclusion: . . . .

. . . .

. . . .

. . . .

I am ready to take the first step forward with this task...

→ Go to **Task Prioritization** worksheet (p.84)

This has been helpful! I want to continue to get to the bottom of why I am procrastinating...

→ Go to **The Avoidance Onion** worksheet (next page)

☆

The Avoidance Onion

You're on this page because you want to explore **what's going on underneath the avoidance** you're feeling right now about a particular thing you have to do. That's great, because the more we peel back the **layers of the avoidance**, the more we're going to get to the heart of what's going on, emotionally.

That's why I call this exercise **The Avoidance Onion**, because just like an onion, avoidance often has **multiple emotional layers** that enclose **one core belief** that is stopping us from moving forward with something. Sometimes, this **core belief** is buried under a lot of layers; other times, we can get right to it, and bring it out to the light very easily.

And when you can bring that core belief out to the light to look at it, it starts to change on its own, simply from intentionally observing it. It makes something that's been hidden visible to us, and, as a result, we can then start to make different decisions about what to do going forward.

Also, sometimes when you peel back the layers on *one* task, you reveal what's holding you back on *many tasks* that you are avoiding doing.

So, let's peel back that **avoidance onion** and see what's underneath.

The Avoidance Onion—Exercise

For this exercise, we're going to explore the different **layers of avoidance** you're feeling about the task you need to do. We write out each layer until we get to the **negative core belief** below. The **negative core belief** is something unfair or unkind that we think about ourselves (e.g., "I'm lazy!" "I'm bad at doing things." "I never get anything right!"). As we learned in the **Extreme Thinking Glasses** exercise (p.116), it typically involves using "harsh words" towards ourselves that we believe to be true.

For example:

Task: *Finishing writing my screenplay.*

Outer layer: *I don't want to do this task because... I am stuck on this particular scene of the script and I don't know where I am going with the plot.*

Second layer: *I think I might be feeling this way because... I don't feel like I'm good with writing dialogue.*

Inner layer: *These feelings come from... Thinking that I should be a better writer by now and know what I am doing at this point in my career.*

Negative core belief: *My negative core belief that is holding me back is: "I am a terrible writer."*

What I can tell myself instead: *"I am learning how to write in a more effective way all the time. Each script I write teaches me something and I learn new skills. When I get to the end of this one, I will have learned a lot more about writing."*

Now it's your turn:

Outer layer: *I don't want to do this task because...*

. . . .

. . . .

. . . .

Second layer: *I think I might be feeling this way because...*

. . . .

. . . .

. . . .

☆

Inner layer: *These feelings come from...*

. . . .

. . . .

. . . .

Negative core belief: *My negative core belief that is holding me back is:*

. . . .

. . . .

. . . .

What I can tell myself instead:

. . . .

. . . .

. . . .

Let's keep going...

→ Go to **Roots of Procrastination** worksheet (next page)

☆

Roots of Procrastination

Like all habits, chronic procrastination is a behavioral pattern that we have developed over time. In this next exercise, let's look at the roots of your procrastination tendencies and try to identify where they came from.

Answer the questions below:

What is your first memory of procrastinating something?

. . . .

. . . .

. . . .

. . . .

. . . .

Who do you think you might have learned to procrastinate from?

. . . .

. . . .

. . . .

. . . .

. . . .

When has procrastination not worked out so well for you in the past? Name a specific memory:

. . . .

. . . .

. . . .

. . . .

. . . .

☆

If you could go back in time and talk to your younger self about procrastination, what would you say?

. . . .

. . . .

. . . .

. . . .

. . . .

What would Future-You tell Today-You about procrastination and how to overcome it right now?

. . . .

. . . .

. . . .

. . . .

. . . .

Give yourself specific steps to take:

. . . .

. . . .

. . . .

. . . .

. . . .

Let's keep going...

→ Go to **What I Can Tell Myself** worksheet (next page)

What I Can Tell Myself

Now that we've found the **inner core belief** that's at the heart of the **avoidance onion**, let's work on telling ourselves some kind, encouraging words to counter this belief a little. If you can't get to a place where you can say something really positive to yourself, just get to a place where you can **soften** what you're saying to yourself in a **gentler way**, as though you're taking to a good friend, or someone you care about that you want to encourage forward. We want to lighten up how we're talking to ourselves about doing the task.

You can even imagine how a **very kind teacher would talk to a little kid**, as this tends to get people in a **gentler and more encouraging** frame of mind.

For example:

Negative core belief	Kinder self-talk
"I don't have the skills to do this."	*"I am learning new things and growing all the time. Each project I finish teaches me how to do something I didn't know before."*
"I'm bad at finishing things."	*"I can take tasks one step at a time. I can go at my own pace as long as I am moving forward in small steps."*
"I'm lazy and I always have been."	*"I have done plenty of things before and I will do plenty of things again. Instead of saying 'lazy' I can say, 'I am feeling exhausted.' I can rest and reset myself and then I will feel like I have more energy."*
"I'm awful at learning new things."	*"I am getting better at figuring things out with each project. I am figuring it out, one step at a time."*

☆

"I want it to be perfect and it isn't anywhere close! And I want it to be done!"

"I can go at my own pace. I can be a little kinder with myself in this way to learn and grow. If I keep going in small steps, I can get there."

Now it's your turn:

Negative core belief

Kinder self-talk

. . . .

. . . .

. . . .

. . . .

. . . .

Now, write out a few **encouraging and kind phrases** you can tell yourself any time you get stuck in the future, to help motivate you to keep going!

What I can tell myself to keep going:

. . . .

. . . .

. . . .

. . . .

. . . .

When it comes to self-talk, it's all about quantity and consistency. We need to repeat these phrases as many times a day as possible, until we start to feel that resistance fading away.

So, put these phrases up somewhere you can see them, and every time you walk by, say them to yourself!

☆

Practice the feelings want to feel, and you can feel them more often.

We can do this by practicing kinder self-talk all day long. At some point, you won't have to practice it as regularly, because it will start to stick and change how you're feeling about yourself, and it will change how you feel about the things you want to do.

You're doing great! Let's keep going...

→ Go to **Motivating Self-Talk** worksheet (next page)

Motivating Self-Talk

Let's practice more motivating self-talk to boost our motivation. Here are some examples of kind and encouraging things you can say to yourself that will make you feel like moving forward:

Keep going: This is your own resiliency talking to you and it is saying, "Keep it up!" "Keep going!" "Keep moving forward a little at a time and you'll get there!"

You've done so much to be proud of: Remind yourself you've done so much already and you'll do more things ahead.

You're learning and growing: This is your inner strength reminding you to keep trying: "I am learning so much with each step I take" and "With every step I take, I am helping myself grow."

You've figured things out: You've figured many things out, you continue to figure things out as they happen, and you'll figure many things out again. You may even think, "I am getting better and better at figuring things out."

Good things can happen in the future: This is where your self-soothing kicks in: "It will be okay," "It will all work out somehow," "Things tend to sort themselves out over time," "I can get to my goal if I just move forward a little at a time."

Look how far you've come: This gives you some perspective on your own journey and how it's been successful in many ways that you might not realize. "Look how far I've come from where I started," "I have made so much progress in so many different areas of my life," and other types of self-reflective phrases can really provide some motivational turbo-boosts.

You are enough: This is where we can reassure ourselves and nurture ourselves by remembering our own worth: "You are enough," "You are good enough the way you are," "You do enough," "You will be enough," and "You are always enough."

☆

Motivational Words = Motivating Emotions

Reading that last list of motivating self-talk phrases, did you start to feel your mood lift just a little bit? Play around with a few of your own; custom-tailor the wording of a few positive phrases, until you start to feel that positive shift happening for you.

Now it's your turn. Pick a few phrases that you liked from those above, or make your own up that "click" on your motivation.

Motivating things I can say to myself:

. . . .

. . . .

. . . .

. . . .

. . . .

. . . .

. . . .

. . . .

Write them out and put them up somewhere you can see them! The more you say them, the more they can motivate you!

Good job!

→ Go to **Different Rules** worksheet (next page)

☆

Different Rules

You've found yourself here because you might be expecting yourself to be "perfect" or to do something "perfectly," without any mistakes or flaws. You may have accidentally set up harsh and unfair rules for yourself that you wouldn't apply to other people.

Often, when we slip into perfectionism, we think "different rules" apply to us than other people, and this can influence how we talk to ourselves in overly critical ways.

An example might be that if someone else makes a mistake, you say something kind and soothing to them:

What I would tell other people: *"That's okay, we can fix this. No one will even notice this tiny mistake. It will all work out."*

vs.

What I tell myself: *"I'm such an idiot and I always screw everything up. Everyone is going to notice I messed this up and they're going to be upset with me. Why am I so bad at things? This is going to be a disaster."*

When we make different rules for other people versus ourselves, it's going to affect our self-esteem, our confidence, and our motivation to finish tasks.

Why wouldn't you talk to yourself in the *same way* as you talk to other people? Why wouldn't you treat yourself with the same kindness that you treat others with? You deserve your own kindness and support, too.

☆

We think if it can't be "perfect," we shouldn't even try. But would we tell another person that they shouldn't try if they can't be perfect? You probably wouldn't talk to another person in this harsh way. If you did, it would be a really unfair, and when you talk to yourself in this way, it's just as unfair.

This exercise challenges to look at **unfair and different rules** you may have formed for yourself. Try to fill out both sides below as honestly as possible, and then take your time to compare the two answers.

Making a mistake:

What I tell other people: *What I tell myself:*

. . . .

. . . .

. . . .

. . . .

Feeling like I'm not getting there fast enough:

What I tell other people who   *What I tell myself:*
feel like this:

. . . .

. . . .

. . . .

. . . .

☆

Worrying about what other people will think:

What I tell other people when they worry: *What I tell myself:*

....

....

....

....

Worrying about succeeding because it might make other people upset/jealous:

What I tell other people when they worry about this: *What I tell myself:*

....

....

....

....

Worrying about failure:

What I tell other people when they worry about this: *What I tell myself:*

....

....

....

....

☆

Worrying that "I didn't do everything right!":

What I tell other people when they worry about this:	*What I tell myself:*
. . . .	. . . .
. . . .	. . . .
. . . .	. . . .
. . . .	. . . .
. . . .	. . . .

Now, reading through your answers, what will you change so that we can make the rules similar instead of different?

. . . .

. . . .

. . . .

. . . .

. . . .

. . . .

How did you develop different rules for yourself vs. other people? When did this start for you? Who taught you to do this for yourself?

. . . .

. . . .

. . . .

. . . .

. . . .

. . . .

☆

Tell yourself why you deserve your own kindness and support from now on:

. . . .

. . . .

. . . .

. . . .

. . . .

. . . .

Conclusion (what you learned from doing this worksheet):

. . . .

. . . .

. . . .

. . . .

. . . .

. . . .

→ Go to **Roots of Perfection** worksheet (next page)

☆

Roots of Perfectionism

For this exercise, let's take a little time explore the roots of our perfectionism. Sometimes, when we're growing up, we learn that we have to compensate for having ADHD by working twice as hard as others. This can create an unfair expectation of ourselves that we need to do things at an extremely high level of execution all the time. Often, this is how the idea of "perfectionism" sneaks in. We believe that if we can do something "perfectly," people will like our performance more or even like us more as a result.

But this is a faulty core belief. We don't have to do things perfectly to have worth and value to ourselves or to others. We have worth just as we are. The things we do have value without having to be perfect. Most of the time, other people aren't expecting you to be perfect or do things perfectly at all; these are just unfair rules we've developed for ourselves that we don't apply to other people.

In this exercise, you can explore where your perfectionism might stem from.

When did the tendency towards perfectionism start?

. . . .

. . . .

. . . .

. . . .

What is your first memory of feeling pressured to do something "perfectly"?

. . . .

. . . .

. . . .

. . . .

☆

If you could go back in time, what would you tell yourself about perfectionism?

. . . .
. . . .
. . . .
. . . .

What would Future-You tell Today-You about overcoming perfectionism right now?

. . . .
. . . .
. . . .
. . . .

Good job!

→ Go to **Facts vs. Feelings** worksheet (next page)

Facts vs. Feelings

Sometimes, when we feel intense and harsh emotions about tasks we need to do, it's easy to **confuse our feelings with facts**. It can be helpful to separate the two for yourself so you can see the difference on paper. Figure out what is an actual fact vs. a feeling you're having for a situation that's making you feel like procrastinating doing something.

For this exercise, write out the strong negative feeling you have about the task you need to do or your ability to do it. Then write the actual facts of the situation. After that, read both and write something encouraging you can tell yourself to remember in the future. In this way, we can balance out our intense feelings with facts.

Here are some examples:

Strong feeling I have: *I am scared that when I actually write this story, everyone will hate it. They will think I am terrible writer.*

Actual facts about the situation: *I actually don't know what people will think. I haven't even written it yet. How can I know that when I haven't written it yet? I don't know the future. Also, many people aren't mean like that towards other people's progress.*

What I can tell myself: *I am imagining a scenario where everything I do is a disaster. In real life, many things I have done have not been disasters. So, I don't really know how this will go, and I can lighten up about it. My feelings aren't facts. I can just tell myself, "Take one step forward and see how it goes after." That way I won't overthink it.*

Strong feeling I have: *I procrastinated mailing in my forms to renew my car registration and now they are late. I feel like an idiot. There is something wrong with me. Nobody else forgets these things.*

Actual facts about the situation: *Other people also forget to mail these* things in; otherwise, they wouldn't have a late fee. They have a fee because it's probably pretty common that people forget to send it in by the deadline. In which case, I would be like a lot of people.

What I can tell myself: *I am not a terrible person because I procrastinated mailing something; I am just human. I can correct the mistake and move on. I might just be expecting to be perfect, and no one is, so I can go a little easier on myself. If someone else did this, I would be understanding and tell them it's not a big deal! I can do that for myself, too.*

Strong feeling I have: *I know I'm going to mess this project up because I don't know what I'm doing and I don't have the skills.*

Actual facts about the situation: *I don't know I'm going to mess it up because I haven't even taken the first step forward yet. I'm "future predicting" instead of just seeing what will happen.*

What I can tell myself: *I don't have to assume the future will be a negative outcome. The only way to get skills is to do things like this and get through them. I will learn as I do it.*

Now it's your turn:

Strong feeling I have:

. . . .

. . . .

. . . .

. . . .

Actual facts about the situation:

. . . .

. . . .

☆

. . . .

. . . .

What I can tell myself:

. . . .

. . . .

. . . .

. . . .

Strong feeling I have:

. . . .

. . . .

. . . .

. . . .

Actual facts about the situation:

. . . .

. . . .

. . . .

. . . .

What I can tell myself:

. . . .

. . . .

. . . .

. . . .

Strong feeling I have:

. . . .

. . . .

. . . .

. . . .

Actual facts about the situation:

. . . .

. . . .

. . . .

. . . .

What I can tell myself:

. . . .

. . . .

. . . .

. . . .

Strong feeling I have:

. . . .

. . . .

. . . .

. . . .

Actual facts about the situation:

. . . .

. . . .

. . . .

. . . .

What I can tell myself:

. . . .

. . . .

. . . .

. . . .

Strong feeling I have:

. . . .

. . . .

. . . .

. . . .

Actual facts about the situation:

. . . .

. . . .

. . . .

. . . .

What I can tell myself:

. . . .

. . . .

. . . .

. . . .

You're doing an amazing job! Let's keep going...

→ Go to **The Encouragement List** worksheet (next page)

☆
The Encouragement List

You've been working on shifting your own self-talk, which is really great to do. In this exercise, you will write down any outside encouragement that you get from external sources, so that you can read it whenever you start to feel stuck again.

For this exercise, write down general encouragement that you've heard that you can read to yourself when you need a little boost to complete something. It can be something someone told you in the past, something they've told you in the present, or something you remember seeing or hearing. You can also include words you've read in inspirational books.

Encouraging words I've heard from others:

. . . .

. . . .

. . . .

. . . .

. . . .

. . . .

Encouraging quotes from books, songs, or movies:

. . . .

. . . .

. . . .

. . . .

. . . .

. . . .

☆

Encouraging words from famous people I admire:

. . . .

. . . .

. . . .

. . . .

. . . .

. . . .

Encouraging words I would like to tell myself right now:

. . . .

. . . .

. . . .

. . . .

. . . .

. . . .

Time to get motivated, let's keep going...

→ Go to **The Finish Line Picture** worksheet (next page)

☆

The Finish Line Picture

Here's an exercise to get us feeling really motivated to complete our goal. Let's **imagine** for a minute that we have crossed the finish line of our project.

Amazing! Congratulations, you did it!

Now, I want you to really imagine how you will *feel* when you complete this task. And then I want you to imagine something fun you will do for yourself as **a reward** for completing this goal. It can be something small, like having a nice cup of tea or going somewhere in nature for a walk. However, for the purposes of this visualization exercise, it should be something **you can do on your own, just for you**. Let's celebrate our successes with ourselves first, before we involve other people in the process. So, invite others along later, for future celebrations, but, for now, let's pick something simple and easy we can do on our own after we finish.

Draw a picture of what you will do to reward yourself after you have crossed the finish line. Be sure to write out the future emotions you want to feel underneath the picture:

☆

How did that visualization feel? Feelings I will feel:

. . . .

. . . .

. . . .

. . . .

. . . .

. . . .

Keep this picture in your mind. Look at it for a few minutes and practice feeling the feelings you want to feel.

You're doing a great job! One more page to go and we'll be on our way to motivating ourselves to take action soon!

→ Go to **Future-You Letter** worksheet (next page)

☆

Future-You Letter

You're now on your way to feeling really motivated just from picturing yourself crossing that finish line on the previous page! When we picture something, we're mentally rehearsing doing it. This is often the mental preparation we need to get our brains in gear to complete our goal.

Next, let's do a powerful exercise that will not only make you feel more motivated, but also has the power to potentially make you feel *happier* for up to six months after you do it!

Researchers at York University in Toronto had participants practice visualizing "a future scene where current issues were resolved" and then instructed participants to imagine giving themselves "advice on how to get there." This resulted in "significant increases in happiness observable at 6 months and significant decreases in depression sustained up to 3 months." Participants who had been high on the self-criticism scale at the start of the study became "happier in only one week's time" after doing this visualization on a regular basis (Shapira and Mongrain 2010).

So, now we're going to write a letter from **Future-You** to **Today-You**, telling you all the ways you're going to overcome this procrastination and get to the finish line with your task or goal.

Remember: Be kind and encouraging to yourself. Tell yourself all the things you can do when those procrastination clouds loom above. Then tell yourself something to inspire you to keep going!

Dear Today-Me,

. . . .

. . . .

. . . .

. . . .

. . . .

☆

. . . .

. . . .

. . . .

. . . .

. . . .

. . . .

. . . .

. . . .

. . . .

. . . .

. . . .

Love,
Future-Me

Wow, that was great!

I need help finding the first step forward now...

→ Go to **Task Prioritization** worksheet (p.84)

I have already broken my steps down, and I am ready to start putting them in my schedule...

→ Go to **Time Blocking** worksheet (p.156)

I want to avoid getting distracted going forward...

→ Go to **Getting Distracted** worksheet (p.153)

Half-Way Drift

You've found yourself on this page because you partially completed a task or project and then "drifted off" into procrastination. Perhaps you started by taking a break that turned into a **"Procrasti-break,"** or perhaps you celebrated completing a task too early, before you were fully done with it.

Let's address this by establishing what "fully done" means for the task or project you're currently stuck on.

Two examples:

Half-Done

Finish last chapters of novel

Fully Done

Turn completed novel into editor

Conclusion *(describe what happened): I think I started celebrating being finished with my novel too soon, felt like it was done, and then I forgot to go back to it for too long.*

New Deadline for Fully Done: *I will start my novel again and finish it in the next three months. I don't have that many pages left to do, I just have to give myself a deadline. My new deadline is by November 30th.*

Half-Done

Ordered rowing machine

Fully Done

Assemble it and move to the spare room.

Conclusion *(describe what happened): I think with the rowing machine, I just really didn't want to assemble it as I don't like putting things together. I don't have a lot of confidence when it comes to following instructions.*

New Deadline for Fully Done: *I will clear some space on Saturday to put it together, and I can watch videos online to help me figure it out. I will build it in the spare room so I won't need to move it afterwards. My new deadline is this Saturday.*

Now it's your turn:

Half-Done

·   ·

·   ·

Fully Done

Conclusion:

· ·

· ·

· ·

· ·

New Deadline for Fully Done:

· ·

· ·

· ·

· ·

Half-Done

Fully Done

·   ·

·   ·

Conclusion:

· ·

· ·

· ·

· ·

☆

New Deadline for Fully Done:

. . . .

. . . .

. . . .

. . . .

Half-Done	Fully Done
. . . .	. . . .
. . . .	. . . .

Conclusion:

. . . .

. . . .

. . . .

. . . .

New Deadline for Fully Done:

. . . .

. . . .

. . . .

. . . .

I need to get motivated to fully complete this task now...

→ Go to **Activation Energy** worksheet (p.96)

I want to learn how to avoid getting distracted in the future...

→ Go to **Getting Distracted** worksheet (next page)

☆

Getting Distracted

You have found yourself on this page because you are **getting distracted** a lot from the task or project that you need to do.

Distractions can be tricky because sometimes we are choosing to do them deliberately, and other times, we're doing them automatically, and we don't even realize that we're distracting ourselves from our main goal.

So, to begin, let's make a list of **"time sinkholes"** we find ourselves falling into frequently, and let's put them into two columns, Visible and Subtle.

For example:

Task: *Answering a large amount of work emails*

Visible Distractions	**More Subtle Distractions**
Play too many games on the computer	Catch myself overthinking too much
Get distracted by doing other work tasks	Check my text messages too often
Scroll through social media for long stretches	Get up to get snacks too frequently

Now it's your turn:

Task: . . . .

Visible Distractions	**More Subtle Distractions**
. . . .	. . . .
. . . .	. . . .
. . . .	. . . .

Good job calling those time sinkholes out! Let's move on...

→ Go to **Where Does Time Go?** worksheet (next page)

Where Does Time Go?

Now that we've sorted out the main offending time sinkholes for you, let's get really honest about how much time each of them is taking.

Pick the **main distractions** from the **Getting Distracted** worksheet, and let's write out **how much time** we are losing approximately **each day and each week** to them. If your time sinkhole is related to your phone, under settings, you can find how much time you are spending on apps.

Underneath, write a conclusion that you came to after completing this exercise.

Here's an example:

Task: *Answering a large amount of work emails*

Main Distractions	Time Per Day	Time Per Week (approx.)
Playing games on my computer	4 hours a day	20 hours per week
Scrolling through social media	2 hours a day	6 hours per week
Overthinking and worrying	at least 2 hours a day	14 hours per week

Conclusion: *I am going to work at noticing when I am starting to do these things more now. To begin with, I will really target cutting down my game playing time by half, until I have caught up on my work emails this week.*

☆

Now it's your turn:

Task: . . . .

Main Distractions	Time Per Day	Time Per Week (approx.)
. . . .	. . . .	. . . .
. . . .	. . . .	. . . .
. . . .	. . . .	. . . .
. . . .	. . . .	. . . .

Conclusion:

. . . .

. . . .

. . . .

. . . .

How did that exercise feel to do? Do you feel like you're ready to take some of that time back now?

→ Go to **Time Blocking** worksheet (next page)

Time Blocking

You have found yourself here because you've broken down your task or goal into small steps. Now you need to schedule it into your calendar. If you haven't broken your task down into small steps yet, go to the **Time Mapping** worksheet first (p.85). You'll need to know what the next weekly step you're taking is before you can proceed with this worksheet.

Moving forward, let's write out the small steps you need to take this week along with how much time they will each take to do.

Note: Give yourself way more than enough time to do each step.

When we give ourselves more than enough time, it decreases the stress of doing the task. When we give ourselves too short a time to do something, it increases the stress of doing the task.

Here's an example:

TASK: *Writing a history paper*

WEEKLY STEPS	TIME
Find books on the subject	*2 hours*
Write an outline of paper	*2 hours*

Now, draw out your time blocks below:

FIND BOOKS
(2 HOURS)

WRITE OUTLINE
(2 HOURS)

Now, looking at your weekly calendar, where you can drop these **two time blocks** into your schedule? You may not want to do them back to back. You may want to leave some spaces in between these boxes for **"time buffer breaks"** where you can reset your mental energy before you continue with other tasks. As everyone's brains are different, find the strategy of arranging your time boxes that works for you.

For example, let's say you take the **first time block** and you put it on Monday from 9 to 11 am in your calendar. You would add it in to your master calendar during this time for this block.

Then, on Tuesday afternoon, you might drop the **second time block** in, from 2 to 4 pm. And maybe you've left yourself some buffer space around each time block so you're not trying to cram these tasks in around many other stressful tasks you need to do.

In your calendar, it might look like this:

TIME	MONDAY	TUESDAY
9.00		
10.00	FIND BOOKS 2 HOURS	
11.00		
12.00		
1.00		
2.00		
3.00		WORK ON OUTLINE 2 HOURS
4.00		
5.00		

☆

Here's another example:

TASK: *Finish organizing my closet*

WEEKLY STEPS	**TIME**
Sort through and store all winter clothes	*3 hours*
Rearrange current spring clothes in a neat and tidy way	*1 hour*

Draw out your time blocks:

SORT WINTER
CLOTHES
(3 HOURS)

ORGANIZE
SPRING
CLOTHES
(1 HOUR)

Then look at your master calendar and drop in each of the time boxes in places that will stress you out the least during the week. Take into consideration other things on your plate and how much energy each of these time boxes will cost you. You may not feel like sorting through clothes after a long day of work, in which case don't drop it in your calendar there.

We want to match the time block with the best space for our own mental energy.

Now, when you're looking at your time blocks, and sorting through clothes for three hours sounds way too exhausting to you (as it would to many people), this is an **internal cue** that we need to break this time block down into smaller blocks. So, we can do this instead:

SORT WINTER
CLOTHES PART 1
(1.5 HOURS)

SORT WINTER
CLOTHES PART 2
(1.5 HOURS)

ORGANIZE
SPRING
CLOTHES
(1 HOUR)

If doing this task seems more reasonable now that it's in smaller chunks, you can move forward with finding space in your calendar for each of these three time blocks. Remember to keep the "stress factor" in mind, and try to go gentler in your approach to scheduling things. Give yourself a lot of breaks. Don't do it all in one long, stressful marathon. Break big things down until they feel manageable, and take into consideration everything else that you have going on.

And now, it's your turn. Give it a try!

TASK: . . . .

WEEKLY STEPS	**TIME**
. . . .	. . . .
. . . .	. . . .
. . . .	. . . .
. . . .	. . . .

Draw out your time blocks in the space below:

☆

Next, look at your master calendar, and try to find places that **best suit your mental energy** to drop in each of your **time blocks**. Leave yourself enough "time buffer breaks" in between things to rest and reset yourself.

Now add your time blocks into your schedule for this week!

Let's move on to get closer to your goal...

→ Go to **Time Tracking** worksheet (next page)

☆

Time Tracking

You've found yourself on this page because you are ready to start tracking your weekly steps towards your goal! That's great, because it means you're feeling more motivated to move forward again. I am so excited for you to cross over that finish line at the end of these pages!

If you haven't broken down your goal into steps yet...

→ Go to **Time Mapping** worksheet (p.85)

If you haven't learned how to put the steps into your calendar...

→ Go to **Time Blocking** worksheet (p.156)

If you've already done all of these things, then let's continue...

Weekly tracking systems can give you that needed accountability to complete your goals. When we track things on paper, we can now see our progress in a visual map before us, and it can really give us a boost of motivation to cross that finish line.

When using a tracking system, consider these guidelines:

▸ Put your tracking journal or calendar somewhere you will notice it throughout the day. It can be helpful if it's on a visible wall or on your desk by your computer.
▸ Don't get stuck on days where nothing happened. Write it down anyway. Tracking doesn't always mean that you finished everything on your to-do list. The act of tracking **any** data is important, so that, over time, you can see the general trajectory of the information you've collected. Think percentages!
▸ Don't beat yourself up! Write stuff down in a simple list form. It takes only about 30 seconds to do. Then move on to something else.
▸ At the end of each month, do a monthly review of your data so that you can take stock of everything you did, and figure out how to avoid obstacles next month.

☆

HABITS: The Calendar Method

If you're tracking a weekly habit, print out a blank calendar sheet for the month and put it somewhere very visible. Each day that you remember to do your habit, mark a RED X on that particular day.

If you skip a day, don't beat yourself up. Just try to start a new RED X streak when you're ready again. The point of this exercise is to overcome the procrastination that most people feel in the first one to three months of starting a new habit. We're looking at the general percentage of RED Xs, so try to avoid getting stuck on any one day that we don't manage to do our habit. This is a long game, not a short one. We have to show ourselves patience and kindness as we move forward across a few months with this tracking system.

It can be helpful to keep this habit calendar going for at least a few months, depending on how hard the habit is for you to do. You will know when you don't need to track it any more. Once the habit has stuck, and you're doing it naturally, you will no longer feel like making the RED X. In the beginning, the RED Xs will be the little daily boosts you need to zoom you across those first weeks and months as you form that new neural pathway for your brain.

See how many you can collect!

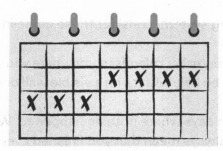

GOALS: The Weekly Tracking Journal

In the pages that follow, you'll learn how to track your weekly progress towards goals and projects using a very simple bullet journaling system.

☆

In the **Weekly Tracking** pages ahead, write down each of the small steps you took towards completing your goal in a short bullet list in the weekly square. Each week, try to simply summarize steps you took, and don't worry if some weeks are slower than others. At the end of the month, answer the review questions and include notes to yourself to remember what to focus on next month. This is also your chance to give yourself a little praise and encouragement for everything you moved forward that month!

For tracking, consistency is key. Try to write down your steps each week as much as possible. After you consistently do this for a few months, you may start to find that you enjoy this new habit. This is often the case for many clients! They resist doing it at first, but after a few months, it starts to become a daily practice that gives them a little motivation boost each time they do it.

Give it a try for at least the next month!

How to use this tracker:

Here's an example of how to fill out the weekly squares for the month. Write out two to five bullet points per week, tracking the current goal or project you are working on.

GOAL/HABIT: Look for a new job

WEEK 1:	**WEEK 2:**
Sent out resumes to three jobs Updated my LinkedIn profile	Had one phone interview

WEEK 3:	**WEEK 4:**
Sent out 2 more resumes Networked at a conference Reached out to a web designer to revamp my website	Set up Zoom interview for the next week

MONTHLY SUMMARY: One interview scheduled, will continue to network and reach out to colleagues next month, will also update my website.

☆

Keep track of your weekly goal progress for the next 3-6 months. At the end of each month, write out a **monthly review** of things you've learned and be sure to give yourself a whole lot of credit and praise for all the steps you've completed!

Let's start tracking...

→ Go to the **next page**

☆

GOAL/HABIT: Look for a new job

WEEK 1:	**WEEK 2:**
WEEK 3:	**WEEK 4:**

MONTHLY SUMMARY: ....
....

Monthly Review

Month:..

Things I am proud of doing this month:

....
....
....
....

☆

Procrastination signs I noticed this month:

. . . .

. . . .

. . . .

. . . .

What I learned this month:

. . . .

. . . .

. . . .

. . . .

What I want to focus on doing next month:

. . . .

. . . .

. . . .

. . . .

I'm done tracking, let's get to the finish line...

→ Go to **The Procrastination Signs** worksheet (p.171)

I'm going to track for another month...

→ Go to **next page**

☆

GOAL/HABIT: Look for a new job

WEEK 1:	**WEEK 2:**
WEEK 3:	**WEEK 4:**

MONTHLY SUMMARY: . . . .

Monthly Review

Month: . . . .

Things I am proud of doing this month:

. . . .

. . . .

. . . .

. . . .

☆

Procrastination signs I noticed this month:

. . . .

. . . .

. . . .

. . . .

What I learned this month:

. . . .

. . . .

. . . .

. . . .

What I want to focus on doing next month:

. . . .

. . . .

. . . .

. . . .

I'm done tracking, let's get nearer the finish line...

→ Go to **The Procrastination Signs** worksheet (p.171)

I'm going to track for another month...

→ Go to next page

☆

GOAL/HABIT: Look for a new job

WEEK 1:	WEEK 2:

WEEK 3:	WEEK 4:

MONTHLY SUMMARY: . . . .

Monthly Review

Month: . . . .

Things I am proud of doing this month:

. . . .

. . . .

. . . .

. . . .

☆

Procrastination signs I noticed this month:

. . . .

. . . .

. . . .

. . . .

What I learned this month:

. . . .

. . . .

. . . .

. . . .

What I want to focus on doing next month:

. . . .

. . . .

. . . .

. . . .

I'm done tracking, let's get to that finish line...

→ Go to **The Procrastination Signs** worksheet (p.171)

I want to complete more of the worksheets in the book before I cross the finish line...

→ Go to **Worksheet Checklist** (p.71)

☆

The Procrastination Signs

How exciting! I see that you're now making your way out of the procrastination fog you were stuck in before. You are on your way to becoming a full-fledged **pro-active procrastination catcher** now, and it's time to review what you've learned so we can get you across that finish line.

Before we get to the end, if you want to return to complete all the worksheets in the book first, you can go to the **Worksheet Checklist** (p.71).

And now, in one last worksheet finale, let's review what we've learned here in this book!

We're going to write out your **procrastination warning signs** so that you can remember how to call them out from now on.

Since everyone behaves in different ways when they are procrastinating, these procrastination warning signs will look different for each person. Take a moment to really think about what you tend to do when you are procrastinating something as you fill out the page below.

Write out what you tend to do when you're procrastinating, and then write out a reason using the word "because."

Examples:

*I tend to buy too many things online **because** shopping reduces my stress.*

*I tend to do a lot of house cleaning instead of working on my paper **because** I think I am being productive, even though I'm avoiding my paper.*

*I stop opening mail **because** opening it means I have to look at it, and I don't want to acknowledge it exists. I pretend the mail isn't there when it isn't open.*

Conclusion: I will be more careful when I catch myself doing too much online shopping in a row or when I choose to clean at strange times in the future. I

☆

also am going to start opening the mail right after I get it from the mailbox from now on, as I know that's a big warning sign for me. I am going to start to observe if these things mean I am procrastinating something going forward.

Now it's your turn:

My procrastination warning signs

(Write out what you tend to do when you're procrastinating and a reason you think you do these things):

. . . .
. . . .
. . . .
. . . .
. . . .
. . . .
. . . .

Conclusion:

. . . .
. . . .
. . . .
. . . .

Now that we've looked at the signs of procrastination, let's try to catch the warning signs of stress...

→ **Almost there!** Go to **The Stress Signs** worksheet (next page)

☆

The Stress Signs

Now, let's look at what **the early signs of stress rising** look like for you. Since stress tends to affect our ability to make decisions and to get stuff done, this worksheet will help you catch your stress so you can pro-actively take steps to lower it, before it gets too high.

Internal stress signs are how stress *feels* inside your body and brain, and **external stress signs** are what *people might observe* you doing when you're at a high level of stress.

Here are some examples:

When I start to feel a high level of stress...

INTERNAL SIGNS
I get headaches.

I can't stop worrying.
I have a lot of trouble focusing.

EXTERNAL SIGNS
I start snapping at people and acting grumpy.
I forget to take a lunch break.
I lose my keys and phone a lot; I can't find things.

Now it's your turn:

INTERNAL SIGNS

. . . .

. . . .

. . . .

. . . .

. . . .

. . . .

EXTERNAL SIGNS

. . . .

. . . .

. . . .

. . . .

. . . .

. . . .

☆

List 3–5 ways you can bring down your stress on a daily basis:

1. ....

2. ....

3. ....

4. ....

5. ....

Keep it up!

→ Go to **next page**

☆

Self-Talk Review

You've been working on your **self-talk** throughout this book and you're doing a great job learning new patterns of thought. And now it's time to put those new self-talk skills to the test in this worksheet.

What are some **"self-talk warning signs"** that we're sliding into overly harsh self-talk towards ourselves? Sometimes, clients will refer to this as "going down the rabbit hole" that leads them to a very "unmotivated" state where they start to procrastinate.

An example of these **self-talk warning signs** might be thoughts like, "I never do anything right," "Nothing I do seems to matter," or "I'll never finish this and I'm way behind already."

What are some **self-talk warning signs** for you that your self-talk is starting to tip in a harsh and critical direction?

Example:

My self-talk warning signs:

"I start telling myself I'm 'lazy' which tends to make me feel really bad like I'll never change. It leads to me beating myself up more."

What will you do when you notice these self-talk signs?

"I can remind myself that I'm doing okay, I'm figuring things out. I can remind myself to go easier on myself. I can remind myself to talk to myself like I would my own friend. I can also remind myself that I've figured out many things before and I will again."

☆

Now it's your turn:

My self-talk warning signs:

. . . .

. . . .

. . . .

. . . .

. . . .

What will you do when you notice these self-talk signs?

. . . .

. . . .

. . . .

. . . .

. . . .

Great job! You're nearly done...

→ Go to **next page**

☆

Accountability Review

Over the course of this book, you've learned the importance of finding accountability and support as you make your way out of the procrastination fog. Let's review and see what we've learned.

What are some ways I can hold myself accountable for moving forward with tasks and goals?

(e.g., *"I will tell my sister my progress from now on by scheduling a weekly phone call,"* body-doubling, daily tracking in a journal)

. . . .

. . . .

. . . .

. . . .

. . . .

. . . .

. . . .

. . . .

What can I tell myself next time I feel like "I have to do everything myself"?

. . . .

. . . .

. . . .

. . . .

. . . .

. . . .

. . . .

. . . .

☆

What can I do when I want to give up half-way through a task or project?

. . . .

. . . .

. . . .

. . . .

. . . .

. . . .

. . . .

How will I remember how much progress I've already made from now on?

. . . .

. . . .

. . . .

. . . .

. . . .

. . . .

. . . .

Just one last worksheet to go...

→ **Go to next page**...you can do it!

☆

The Procrastination Round-Up

You've almost completed your journey through this book and you're nearing the end! I really hope that procrastination fog is starting to lift for you.

To celebrate, let's do one **final round-up** of everything you have learned in this book!

What I have learned about my procrastination tendencies?

. . . .

. . . .

. . . .

. . . .

. . . .

. . . .

. . . .

. . . .

What are some strategies I learned that I can use in the future?

. . . .

. . . .

. . . .

. . . .

. . . .

. . . .

. . . .

☆

What are my main procrastination warning signs (what you are doing that lets you know you're procrastinating)?

. . . .
. . . .
. . . .
. . . .
. . . .
. . . .

What are the "sneakier" types of procrastination that I don't always catch myself doing?

. . . .
. . . .
. . . .
. . . .
. . . .
. . . .

What are the more visible types of procrastination that I tend to do?

. . . .
. . . .
. . . .
. . . .
. . . .
. . . .

☆

How can I catch procrastination earlier from now on?

. . . .

. . . .

. . . .

. . . .

. . . .

. . . .

Write out a few kind and encouraging phrases you will tell yourself from now on:

. . . .

. . . .

. . . .

. . . .

. . . .

. . . .

Write out a few key things you want to remember from this book:

. . . .

. . . .

. . . .

. . . .

. . . .

. . . .

Wow! You did it! I knew you could! How do you feel?

→ **Finally,** on to the **next page**

☆

THE FINISH LINE

**Congratulations! You have completed
your journey through this book.**

From now on, you are officially a **pro-active procrastination catcher**.

You know too much now to let yourself get lost in a fog for too long again.

I hope you have learned new tools that have helped
you navigate out of that procrastination fog you were
feeling so lost in at the beginning of this book.

You did a great job!

Let yourself feel proud of yourself for everything
you've learned in this book.

You've shown a lot of courage taking in all these new skills and tools.

You're figuring it out one step at time.

Keep going! You're making your way out of the fog now
and it will be much smoother sailing ahead...

☆

Should you ever need a map again, simply revisit these
worksheets at the starting line and try a new path.

The more you practice catching procrastination,
the less it can catch you off-guard again.

You've got this!

About the Author

Risa Williams is a licensed psychotherapist, a time management consultant, and the award-winning author of *The Ultimate Time Management Toolkit, The Ultimate Self-Esteem Toolkit, The Ultimate Anxiety Toolkit,* and *Get Stuff Done Without the Stress*. She's also a professor of psychology, a writer, and a busy mom of two. She's been interviewed and featured in many worldwide publications including *Forbes Magazine, Women's World, Wired, Business Insider, Very Well Mind, Psych Central, Therapist Magazine, HuffPost,* and *Real Simple*. Her books have won three national awards including the Living Now Book Award, and her podcast, *The Motivation Mindset*, received the Positive Change Podcast Award.

To learn more, please visit risawilliams.com and follow her on Instagram @risawilliamstherapy. She enjoys hearing from readers—feel free to reach out to her through her website or Instagram.

Mental Health Resources

ADHD resources

ADDitude: www.additudemag.com/category/adhd-add

ADHD self-test: https://add.org/adhd-test

CHADD (Children and Adults with Attention-Deficit/Hyperactivity Disorder): https://chadd.org

Dr. Hallowell, ADHD podcast, resources, and videos: https://drhallowell.com

Stress-reduction strategies

American Institute of Stress: www.stress.org

Box breathing: https://psychcentral.com/health/box-breathing

Psychotherapist directories in the USA

Psychology Today: http://psychologytoday.com

Therapy Den: http://therapyden.com

Psychotherapist directories in the UK

Counselling Directory: www.counselling-directory.org.uk

NHS: www.nhs.uk/service-search/find-a-psychological-therapies-service

Anxiety and mental health resources

ADAA (Anxiety & Depression Association of America): https://adaa.org

American mental health hotlines/NAMI (National Alliance on Mental Illness): www.nami.org/Support-Education/NAMI-HelpLine/Top-HelpLine-Resources

Anxiety UK: www.anxietyuk.org.uk

Mind helpline: www.mind.org.uk/information-support/helplines

Mental health charities

Attention Deficit Disorder Organization: https://add.org

Brain & Behavior Research Foundation: www.bbrfoundation.org

References

Adams, D. (2002) *Salmon of Doubt*. New York, NY: Harmony Books.

Akimbekov, N.S. and Razzaque, M.S. (2021) "Laughter therapy: A humor-induced hormonal intervention to reduce stress and anxiety." *Current Research in Physiology 4*, 135–138. doi:10.1016/j.crphys.2021.04.002

American Institute of Stress (2022) "What is stress?" https://www.stress.org/what-is-stress

Balban, M.Y., Neri, E., Kogon, M.M., Weed, L., *et al.* (2023) "Brief structured respiration practices enhance mood and reduce physiological arousal." *Cell Reports Medicine 4*, 1, 100895. doi:10.1016/j.xcrm.2022.100895

Can, Y.S., Iles-Smith, H., Chalabianloo. N., Ekiz, D., *et al.* (2020) "How to relax in stressful situations: A smart stress reduction system." *Healthcare 8*, 2, 100. doi:10.3390/healthcare8020100.

Cherry, K. (2022, September 3) "How listening to music can have psychological benefits." *Very Well Mind*. www.verywellmind.com/surprising-psychological-benefits-of-music-4126866

Cleveland Clinic (2023) "What is time blindness? And why does it happen?" https://health.clevelandclinic.org/time-blindness

Creswell, J.D., Dutcher, J.M., Klein, W.M., Harris, P.R., and Levine, J.M. (2013) "Self-affirmation improves problem-solving under stress." *PLOS ONE 8*, 5, e62593. doi:10.1371/journal.pone.0062593

Gallup (2019) *Gallup Global Emotions*. Washington, DC: Gallup. https://cdn.cnn.com/cnn/2019/images/04/25/globalstateofemotions_wp_report_041719v7_dd.pdf

Hunt, M.G., Marx, R., Lipson, C., and Young, J. (2018) "No more FOMO: Limiting social media decreases loneliness and depression." *Journal of Social & Clinical Psychology 37*, 10, 751–768. doi:10.1521/jscp.2018.37.10.751

Jaffe, E. (2013) "Why wait? The science behind procrastination." Association for Psychological Science. www.psychologicalscience.org/observer/why-wait-the-science-behind-procrastination

Jabr, F. (2013, October 15) "Why your brain needs more downtime." *Scientific American*. www.scientificamerican.com/article/mental-downtime

Jellineck, M.S. (2010) "Don't let ADHD crush children's self-esteem." MD Edge. www.mdedge.com/psychiatry/article/23971/pediatrics/dont-let-adhd-crush-childrens-self-esteem

Kok, B.E., Coffey, K.A., Cohn, M.A., Catalino, L.I., *et al.* (2013) "How positive emotions build physical health: Perceived positive social connections account for the upward spiral between positive emotions and vagal tone." *Psychological Science* 24, 7, 1123–1132. doi:10.1177/0956797612470827

Lackschewitz, H., Hüther, G., and Kröner-Herwig, B. (2008) "Physiological and psychological stress responses in adults with attention-deficit/hyperactivity disorder (ADHD)." *Psychoneuroendocrinology 33*, 5, 612–624. doi:10.1016/j.psyneuen.2008.01.016

Low, K. (2023) "12 ways to deal with chronic procrastination." *Very Well Mind.* www.verywellmind.com/overcoming-chronic-procrastination-20390

Newberg, A. and Waldman, M. (2012) "Why this word is so dangerous to say or hear." *Psychology Today.* www.psychologytoday.com/us/blog/words-can-change-your-brain/201208/why-word-is-so-dangerous-say-or-hear

Oguchi, M., Takahashi, T., Nitta, Y., and Kumano, H. (2021) "The moderating effect of attention-deficit hyperactivity disorder symptoms on the relationship between procrastination and internalizing symptoms in the general adult population." *Frontiers of Psychology 12*, 708579. doi:10.3389/fpsyg.2021.708579

Oppong, T. (2017) "Psychological secrets to hack your way to better life habits." Observer. https://observer.com/2017/03/psychological-secrets-hack-better-life-habits-psychology-productivity

Rinaldi, A.R., Roper, C.L., and Mehm, J. (2021) "Procrastination as evidence of executive functioning impairment in college students." *Applied Neuropsychology: Adult 28*, 6, 697–706. doi:10.1080/23279095.2019.1684293

Shapira, L.B. and Mongrain, M. (2010) "The benefits of self-compassion and optimism exercises for individuals vulnerable to depression." *Journal of Positive Psychology 5*, 5, 377–389. doi:10.1080/17439760.2010.516763

Sirois, F.M. (2023) "Procrastination and stress: A conceptual review of why context matters." *International Journal of Environmental Research and Public Health 20*, 6, 5031. doi:10.3390/ijerph20065031

Strohmeier, C.W., Rosenfield, B., DiTomasso, R.A., and Ramsay, J.R. (2016) "Assessment of the relationship between self-reported cognitive distortions and adult ADHD, anxiety, depression, and hopelessness." *Psychiatry Research 238*, 153–158. doi:10.1016/j.psychres.2016.02.034

Tseng, J. and Poppenk, J. (2020) "Brain meta-state transitions demarcate thoughts across task contexts exposing the mental noise of trait neuroticism." *Nature Communications 11*, 1, 3480. doi:10.1038/s41467-020-17255-9

University of the West of England (2018, May 4) "Coloring reduces stress and boosts creativity." Neuroscience News. https://neurosciencenews.com/coloring-stress-creativity-8969

Weissenberger, S., Schonova, K., Büttiker, P., Fazio, R., *et al.* (2021) "Time perception is a focal symptom of attention-deficit/hyperactivity disorder in adults." *Medical Science Monitor 27*, e933766-1–e933766-5. doi:10.12659/MSM.933766

White, M.P., Elliott, L.R., Grellier, J., and Economou, T. (2021) "Associations between green/blue spaces and mental health across 18 countries." *Scientific Reports 11*, 1, 8903. doi:10.1038/s41598-021-87675-0